PROVENCE

Books by Lawrence Durrell

PROVENCE

Lawrence Durrell

ARCADE PUBLISHING • NEW YORK

Dedicated to Françoise Kestsman,
magnificent in her generosity and
her beauty

FIRST ARCADE PAPERBACK EDITION 1994

Originally published in hardcover under the title *Caesar's Vast Ghost: Aspects of
Provence*

ISBN 1-55970-247-8
Library of Congress Catalog Card Number 94-70873
Library of Congress Cataloging-in-Publication information is available.

Published in the United States by Arcade Publishing, Inc., New York

Distributed by Little Brown and Company

10 9 8 7 6 5 4 3 2 1

BP
Designed by API

PRINTED IN THE UNITED STATES OF AMERICA

Contents

"A travers le côté Tartarin et le côté Daumier du pays si drôle, où les bonnes gens ont l'accent que tu sais, il y a tant de grec déjà, et il y a la Vénus d'Arles comme celle de Lesbos et on sent encore cette jeunesse-là malgré tout. Je n'en doute pas le moins du monde qu'un jour toi aussi tu connaîtras le Midi."*

— Vincent van Gogh to his brother Theo,
Arles, September 1888

*Translation on page 200

Constrained by history

To thank Mary J. Byrne for her collaboration

1

Constrained by history, now he shall not make
New friendships or attachments
For the circle of the old is closing in . . .
He will simply get beyond the need to explain
How his bounds were set by his mother's dying,
How his comet rose from the coffin of his father's striving:
Lucky indeed is he to have come so far alive,
In an epoch of wars, waging only total peace:
No luckier than to inherit the Golden Fleece.

The secret of whose code engenders peace!

2

He will cure his feelings of the world as threat,
Knitting poems from them, true and mouse-compact;
Find a tellurian delight in the sweeter
Arrow-faithful love-act, having been half girl
And boy, husband and wife in the ancient love-contract.
By the belly-button of Tiresias he will swear,
Or the pineal eye, the pine-cone which made him first aware
Of everything outside the bazaars of the mind.
Only to seek, they said, and ye shall find!

The thrilling yoga of love's double-bind!

Provence

3

Beyond the gossip of the senses' codes,
He'll become at last one of the Heavenly Ones
Who smile and wage silence up there, finger to lip,
With their help he will give time the slip
And join them soon in their heavenly abodes.
Great mysteries undivulged must always be,
Housed in their silence undeviatingly;
Though you a whole infinity may take
You'll not unravel the entire mosaic.

4

One link, the couple, only death can sever,
Conflating man and wife now and for ever.
Old men with ocean-going eyes, fully aware,
Smelling of camp-fire wisdom, the elect,
Their world of shyness beckons like a snare,
Their silence something we can not dissect.
They know, we know, the stealth of human prayer
Whose poisoned fictions beg for our consent,
Reducing loving to this point-event,
Makes here and now a simple everywhere
The human heart was well designed to care.

5

So now all time is winding down to die
In soft lampoons of earthly grace set free:
She is not far to seek, your Cupid's sigh,
Forms like old carotids of ruins to be
Genetics of the doubts love cannot free
In you awake tonight, my love, awake like me.

Introduction

My own version of Provence is necessarily partial and personal, for, like everyone else, I came here to fall in and out of love long ago, entering old Provence by the winding roads, the only ones, the old *Routes Nationales*, down the interminable corridors of cool planes in leaf, at the turn of the harvest moon . . . Memory has kept such versions astonishingly fresh in their warmth and candour. She was waiting there, another writer in travail, waiting at the old Hôtel d'Europe in Avignon with her unfinished manuscript on the Troubadours.

Swerving down those long dusty roads among the olive groves, down the shivering galleries of green leaf I came, diving from penumbra to penumbra of shadow, feeling that icy contrast of sunblaze and darkness under the ruffling planes, plunging like a river trout in rapids from one pool of shadows to the next, the shadows almost icy in comparison with the outer sunshine and hard metalled blue sky. So to come at last upon Valence where the shift of accent begins: the cuisine veers from cream to olive oil and spices in the more austere dietary of the south, with the first olives and mulberries and the tragic splash of flowering Judas, the brilliant violet brushstroke of unique Judas. Here, like the signature at the end of a score, the steady orchestral drizzle of cicadas: such strange sybilline music and such an exceptional biography, so scant of living-time, with so long underground in the dark earth before rising into the light! Anisette (pastis) everywhere declared itself as the ideal accompaniment for the evening meditations of the players of *boules*; no village square in summer was without the clickety-click of the little steel balls, no shady village without its *boulistes* steeped in the Socratic austerity of the silence between throws. The holy silence of the *bouliste* is pregnant with futurity, his convulsions and contortions when things go wrong are pure early cinema; the immortality of Pagnol is based upon a careful study of the graphic originals available to him in a long lifetime of attending tournaments in town and hamlet alike.

Somewhere near St-Rémy

A garage in such a village, say,
Run by a Claude Girofle
And one pig-tailed daughter, Espionnette,
Who mans the pumps with fervour,
Ici on vous sert,
Ici on vous berce!

The souls of temple cats
Eyes like vitreous bubbles
Blown in glass, gypsy eyes,
The faces Plato calls "of a demonic order"
Demons distributing liquid flame.

Unaware of the Druids' ancient charter,
The magical primacy of wishing,
The glands of fire,
Sunshine has carried love away —

2

Lawrence Durrell

At full moon everyone seems right
Or so the water seems to say,
The wanton Pleiades pining for the day!

When I first set foot in Provence one could buy a *mazet* very cheaply — happily for us, for we were broke, the common history of writers. A *mazet* is usually the dependancy of a *mas* (the word itself is the diminutive of *mas*, which means farm or domaine). The tiny *mazet* we bought a few kilometres outside Nîmes afforded us little more than an elementary shelter from the elements. But with industry and hard thinking we transformed it rapidly into a comfortable, indeed snug cottage. I encircled it with dry-stone walls, using the simple garrigue stone which flakes and trims into convenient soup-plate sizes, ideal for walls and balconies. I set this off with a small patio, the girdles of stone showing up the venerable almond trees to perfection. Here we lounged away the golden afternoons and evenings like Chinese philosophers, debating endlessly the hypothetical book which we knew would never be written — the book which contained the essential insights about the place. A compendium of poetic inklings — all that the Ideal Traveller should know!

The winters we spent in the ruined and ruinous old château of Aldo not far from Beaucaire were a real delight until the weather broke; technically we had all enlisted as casual labour for the vine-harvest but, weather permitting, we tended to linger through until October when the olives came up, and then more sporadic harvests like truffles or chestnuts in the nearby forests . . . Since the old pile was quite unheatable by modern means, we tended to use wood for fuel, and do most of our cooking on the embers which piled high in the gigantic Templar fireplace on the ground floor of the keep. And drink. And drink. And drink . . .

And this is how we came by the idea of a book — a book which would not only enshrine our most memorable

3

thoughts but also help us cut down on the calamitous intake of scarlet Fitou (*douze degrés*) or — wilier but no less hazardous for the hand with the pruning-hook — red Corbières. In vain, though we did manage to pile up a mountain of matter, mostly in the form of unanswerable questions about the Roman Thing and the Greek, not to mention the Crusader Thing and the Troubadour Thing. As for the wine, Aldo consoled us with a home-grown thought which he inscribed on the title page of our commonplace book: "Everything really desirable has come about because of, or in spite of, wine!"

Needless to say, all the pious hopes for a wiser policy remained unanswered, just as the book has remained formally unwritten, though the project lacked neither time nor reading nor debate which often turned to open acrimony as one or other of the friends produced some new theory as to the "real nature" of Provence: something inescapably true — so true as to carry conviction!

In vain! In vain! In vain!

We had been elaborating in our minds a conventional travel book of a statutory order — some history, some myth, some insights and striking metaphors appropriate to the glorious landscape, the whole fitted out with appropriate tourist information . . . But the new realization inclined us to believe that the true vision of the place would result in something far more abstract, in a form far less school-bookish. One had begun to realize that while the conventional boundaries created by mountains and rivers resulted in hampered journeys between states and tribes, so that for centuries great ignorance must have prevailed about the habits and beliefs of even quite near neighbours, nevertheless a tenuous contact was always evident. After all, even in such remote epochs as the age of Pythagoras, there are records of contact with the Druids in Britain, and of an exchange of religious and philosophic ideas. And the Roman ruins of, say, Orange seem to echo as if in stony parody those of Epidauros, though how

4

different Greek theatre is from Roman. The heartbeat of a place is recorded in these stone experiences. In the marbles of the Acropolis you can read the eloquent stone echo evolved by Rome in Provence, the sweet Maison Carrée of Nîmes which still carries the code of place, the blood-stroke of Greece's brilliant insight into human unhappiness and the problems of the evolved identity: all this filtered through the Roman wish to excel the race which made them feel aesthetically *parvenus* (which of course they were in terms of their coarseness of vision), while even today in the streets of Arles you will find in the blazing beauty of an Arlésienne, a Roman echo in flesh.

Yet there are surprises for us even here, for even a functional artefact like the Pont du Gard is so huge in conception that its magniloquence is the equal of Westminster Abbey. But we must remember that it was dedicated to water, and water was a God. The best description of the Pont is by Rousseau. It took a great deal to shut a man like him up, but the emergence of this mastodon from the featureless garrigues which house the spring that feeds it deprived him of coherent speech, so uncanny did it seem. It is the size, of course, as well as the realization that the whole construct is slotted together in pieces of honey-coloured stone without the help of mortar. Each individual block is the size of a motor-car! How did the Roman engineers manage to raise these vast chunks so high into the air? But water was precious, water was life, and the Roman was uxorious to a fault about land and its fruits. Provence signified something liked married plenty! The sun determines everything that grows, while water becomes an all-important symbol, a legendary factor because of its capricious changes of level, its sudden shortages, its quick alternations of drought and flood. Water plays on the dry river-beds as if on a giant keyboard, forever shifting its levels, forever hunting in the dry mountains, as if in a hollow tooth, for profounder depths.

For much of what follows I am indebted to idle conversations with my two first friends, Jérôme the saintly tramp and Aldo the aristocrat and vine-grower in his tumbledown château. Theirs is the constant presence without which no poetic evocation of Provence could for me be possible. Thanks to them — I see them now loafing about among the olives, glass in hand, full of Fitou — I can honestly say I have experienced the country with my feet as well as my tongue: long walks and longer potations have characterized my innocent researches, the ideal way to gain access to a landscape so full of ambiguities and secrets. Yes, secrets black with wine, and gold with honey, landscapes of an almost brutal serenity piled one upon another with quixotic profusion, as if to provoke the historic confrontations which have made them significant, muddling up the sacred and the profane, the trivial and the grandiose with operatic richness, mesmerizing one!

In the first euphoria of this therapeutic project, the projected book which they had christened *A Complete Provence* had a certain sweeping insolence which I found commendable. Provence! What was it exactly? In my sleep I often reopen the question and restate it. The tremendous variety of topic is daunting, and when I came to examine the historical data which composes the place's rich history I realized that to do anything with pretensions to completeness would require a dozen volumes! They had given up after a few pages. Could I hope to do otherwise, even by using more impressionistic terms of reference, a system of poetical collage, say? To capture the poetic quiddity of this extraordinary cradle of romantic dissent without sentimentalizing it — for its romantic heart shelters a gorgeous brutality and extremism!

Now, Aldo and Jérôme have vanished from the scene . . . and with them others who have also stolen away into history leaving memories of a Provençal visitation: Henry Miller, Denis de Rougemont, Giono, Marie M-D . . . Sometimes I feel I have been left to complete this book before joining them! Moreover, that I must be careful to register the timbre of Denis's laughter and the famous enthusiasms of a Miller who was full of echoes from Greece . . .

What remains is the work of selection.

Route Saussine 15

Only of late have I come to see this house
As something poisoned when I paid for it;
Its beauty was specious and it hid pure grief.
Your absence, dearest, brings it no relief.
We have all died here; one by spurious one
Of indistinct diseases, lack of sun, or fun,
Or just our turn came up, now mine; so be it, none
Decline into oblivion without a guide,
The last of maladies, death, love can provide
The abandoned garden, dried up fountain oozes,
A stagnant fountain full of tiny frogs
Like miniature Muses; say to yourself
No hope of change with death so near.
Days come and sigh and disappear.
Despair camps everywhere and my old blind dog
Though lacking a prostate pisses everywhere.

– I –

After Valence

To begin with, Provence seemed to be less of a geographical entity than an idea. It was Caesar, after all, who christened it "The Province," and at first its shifting contours, expanding and contracting in response to wars and migrations, seemed to encompass a land-mass which included Geneva on the one hand and Toulouse on the other: an improbably vast territory. But it did not stay stable in the face of history, and slowly its outlines hovered and contracted until it assumed the outlines of our modern Provence which comprises Montélimar in the north, Nice in the east and Béziers or Narbonne in the south . . .

This modern version of this semi-mythical country is roughly what the modern traveller encounters when he strikes directly south from Valence. The Mediterranean suddenly begins to assert itself and the traditional Provençal folklore, the old tourist keyboard, is there with its cypresses and roasted tile roofs, with its ivy and honeysuckle, sycamore and serene plane trees tracing the course of secret rivers hollowed out by the steady drive of the Swiss glaciers in their descent to the sea. The Rhône! But nothing can do fair justice to the light — neither camera nor brush. It has a felicity and eloquence beyond all praise. These skies — the special wounded blue one finds sometimes in Mantegna's skies — are unique to Provence, for they are neither Greek nor Roman. They seem so freshly minted that the peasant faces you encounter in the Saturday market-place have all the poise and gravity of Roman medallions.

But within the last fifteen years much has been changed. All history has been compromised by the deliberate policy of transforming the backward sections of Provence into tourist playgrounds of a sophistication to match Nice and Monte Carlo. In the south, the rather disappointing seaside towns and beaches have been transformed into a ragged hinterland of skyscrapers, a playground for the northern tourists on whom the economy of the region has come largely to depend. Meanwhile the grave housing crisis which followed the Algerian war has provided the peaceable Roman towns of Avignon, Nîmes, Montpellier, Marseille, Béziers and Narbonne with vast unwelcome dormitory suburbs and a wilderness of secondary roads which necessitate a whole new strategy on the part of the tourists who nevertheless still flock to the Midi in search of the sun-drenched amenities promised by the guides.

To this end handsome motorways have been thrown down to replace the modest secondary roads of the past — inadequate for modern traffic. Yes, the new autoroutes have subdued and banalized much wild country. To achieve them with minimum damage, the engineers cut down only one side of the roads' beautiful avenues of plane trees, giving the landscape a sad, defrocked look. And of course they have widened the roads, to the detriment of the old intimacy and charm. With trees shorn, the roads, or at least the major ones, look like handsome women with heads half shaved waiting in a cancer ward for a brain operation with skulls duly marked up in chalk for incisions yet to come! The modern tourist dawdles across this landscape along roads more numerous than in Roman times, roads crowded with his fellows. In fact the new autoroutes have created a new dismay, making one feel that Provence from now on must evolve a new sort of strategy for its visitors, if only because you can now slide from end to end of the country without seeing a single town or treasure, and out the other side into Spain in a single day. All the key spots have been bypassed, while the sleepy old towns like famous Avignon, Arles, Montpellier, have been driven frantic by the importunities of motorists hunting for parking spaces, and have begun digging out an extensive underground system of parking which bids fair to transform tourism in a new way.

It is obvious that the country is a funnel through which almost every race, ancient and modern, has marched either towards or away from, a war; marched upon roads traced and defended by the bravery and enterprise of the ancient Greeks and Romans. Even today it still bears the imprint of their visitation. Although the present period is one of jostle and uncertainty and stress, I am sure that the appearance of the first great Roman thoroughfares provoked much the same sort of shock and uncertainty as the new network of autoroutes, as well as radically modifying the flow of transport both northward and southward. Communications are the key to all change in terms of commercial dealings and the cultures which flower from them. But today a whole new technique is needed to do what one once did by horse or bicycle (some obstinate Swiss and Germans still do) in order to examine the ancient sites which still star the land in all their poetic splendour. Paradoxically enough, they are if anything somewhat less accessible than in the past. So much for progress — the motor-car has swallowed us whole! Aldo, who likes looking on the gloomy side of things, even adds that "the introduction of the compulsory seat-belt for motorists has taken all the fun out of sex!" I quote the opinion for what it is worth . . .

And the tourist offices tend to strike an exultant note, faith-

fully reminding you that you are now passing through Cé-
zanne country . . . It's like asking you to admire an X-ray of
one of the artist's paintings! Yes, there are disappointments
in store, but happily the innate purity and dignity of Provence, particularly the villages and the countryside, will rise
triumphantly above these factors and lift you with them. It
is only in a few places that you will come across gross parodies
of Manhattan or the suburbs of the industrial north. But despite such dispiriting interludes the land still lives, still
breathes . . .

*   *   *

I recall one among many a dramatic occasion when I came
into Provence from the north with autumn well on the way,
driving into a countryside exhausted but replete after a successful harvest of grapes. The vineyards were stripped already, and the burly little crucifixes of vines had already
responded to a freak snowfall with all their charcoal blackness
and their withered forms . . . They had their feet in snow.
Nothing more to expect, one felt, until spring came round
again with the first stealthy green leaves.

The tiny village of Lauret offered me two striking tableaux,
its roofs snow-capped despite bright sunlight. Before one
house the owner had set out a table with a white cloth and
a solitary bottle and glass, to show that he was prepared to
serve the traveller a *table d'hôte* from his own table for a modest
price. The bottle of rosy Pic St-Loup had the corkscrew standing in the cork, the primal eloquence of the new wine setting
up animal thirsts in the passers-by. At the other end of the
village there had been a death, and outside the front door of
a similar style of house stood another table, clothed in black,
on which stood the traditional book to be signed as a mark
of sympathy by the mourners and friends of the deceased.
The candle dripped on to the black cloth. The contrast with
the white snowscape was striking, the juxtaposition of the

two tables fearfully congruent — symbolic of what Provence stood for in terms of human destiny, Mediterranean destiny, linking in one mood the messages carried by ancient Greece and Rome alike. Life and death in the same glass, so to speak!

*　　*　　*

(Whole peoples form their personalities around what they believe, and there are those who recognize that the primal condition in nature is one of impermanence. They practise anchoring their minds in its flux as the basis for a coherent philosophic life. The moral posture in the matter of death is most important. But one feels that real bliss, the smiling silence of pure transcendence, is Asiatic.)

*　　*　　*

The best way to strike up an acquaintance with one of these Provençal towns is to arrive around daybreak, preferably on a market day when the place is full of sleepy vendors unloading their vans and trucks of everything you can imagine from pigeons and hams to olives and plums. The whole town seems to be stretching and yawning and waiting for the sunrise to warm it up. Only the early morning bistros are open but there is many a lesson to be learned, for the market people are specialists in the early morning nip — a swift stab of some neat alcohol to set the wheels of commerce turning. In the smoking bistro you will observe certain elderly traders who greet the dawn with a classic glass of *marc* or cherry brandy or port or a *canon* of red wine. Perhaps others will only settle for a caressing dose of Armagnac or pepper vodka . . . In my own case I recall a visit with Jérôme which was made memorable by the discovery of a singular drink called Arquebuse, which he claimed was harmless yet agreeable. I was given a full wine glass of this product which looked somewhat like vodka or gin. The morning was a trifle cool. I somewhat imprudently drained the glass. When I picked myself up off the floor I asked politely if I might examine the bottle in which this prodigious firewater was delivered to the world. The letterpress which accompanied the drink was highly suggestive. It informed me that what I had just tasted was not an alcohol but, strictly speaking, a "vulnerary," which had been invented in the Middle Ages for use on the battlefields. The recent invention of the Arquebuse had had a marked effect on warfare, causing a new type of flesh wound, more grievous than the arrow wounds known in the past. The doctors of the day welcomed the invention of this stanching and cleansing "vulnerary." But at some point (the bottle does not say when or how) somebody must have sucked his bandage, and from then on there was no looking back; Arquebuse found its place among the more powerful firewaters available to man, ordinary man, and indeed a comfort to all humanity. It appears to be a specific for everything except receding hair, and I know a number of people who swear by it, and always keep a bottle in the larder in order to save lives when need be. This is the kind of information one gathers if one gets up early enough and arrives with the first dawn light in a Provençal town.

Another occasion, which I found somewhat unexpected and disconcerting, but which seemed rather typical of meridional procedures, turns upon the enigmatic behaviour of an introspective-looking individual sitting alone in a secluded corner of a popular bistro. The waiter began a prolonged handout of free doses of Armagnac to all and sundry — a most welcome act of generosity on a chilly morning. Moreover, no sooner was one glass emptied than another appeared in its place and it was clear that if we were not careful we would be in for a prolonged binge. I had, of course, read all about meridional hospitality to strangers, and dutifully toasted my host by raising my glass before draining it. But when the second glass appeared and it became clear that there would be more to follow, I became intrigued enough to

wonder what he could be celebrating in such exemplary fashion. (I adore Armagnac, but I was also at the wheel of the
car that day.) I could not resist asking the waiter who the
gentleman in the corner was, and what he was celebrating.
"Has he won the lottery or broken the bank at the casino?"
The waiter shook his head and said, "Much better than that.
He has been a martyr for years to a most persistent tapeworm.
He has tried everything without avail. But today the head
came away and he passed it. *Ça se fête, n'est-ce pas?*"

*   *   *

I began to see the outlines of the sort of book Aldo and Jérôme
were pleading for: "It could be quite small like The Philosopher's Stone" (Aldo), yet momentous in its significance for
the right sort of traveller — a translation of that poetic figment
we have christened "Provence," a symbol of glamour and
human romance. A simple roll-call of the great historic personages who have passed this way . . . an extraordinary gallery of human types, linking a Caesar or a Hannibal to a
Dante or a Petrarch; warriors, historians, philosophers and
poets. A compendium of poetic references through which
one might traverse Greek and Roman history, touching salient
historic flashpoints which rise out of time and circumstance
like atolls from the ocean of the past.

One recalls Nikos Kazantzakis gazing at the pediment of
the temple of Zeus at Olympia and remarking, "The great
artist looks beneath the flux of everyday reality and sees eternal, unchanging symbols . . . he takes ephemeral events and
relocates them in an undying atmosphere . . . This is why
not only the sculptors but all the great artists of classical
Greece, wishing to ensure the perpetuation of every contemporary memorial to victory, relocated history in the elevated
and symbolic atmosphere of myth. Instead of representing
contemporary Greeks warring against the Persians, they gave
us the Lapithae and centaurs . . . Thus a historic event, oc-

14

curring at a specific time, escaped time and bound itself to the entire race and that race's ancient visions."

So we babbled and boozed our way towards whatever *fête votive* lay ahead on the crowded calendar of the Provençal year. For a while, too, we had itinerant visitors who gave a fugitive variety to our discussions and enriched our social life as wine-tasters, drinkers, drainers . . . Indeed, wine-lore was the axis around which much of our lives revolved. Aldo, for example, would have long since traded in his vast unmanageable, unheatable château at St-Chaptes had it not been for the excellent vineyards which surrounded it. They produce a robust black wine which has made its quiet way to the front rank of the local brews. In our private gossip we refer to it as Old Iniquity (*Grand Cru des Solitaires et des Introspectifs*), though in the trade its official title is Pic Ste-Barbe, a local mountain. It brought in enough to enable Aldo to hang on to his grandiose family home.

Here, too, were many merry meetings — a painter, a defrocked priest, a novelist, myself, Jérôme and Aldo, two girls from a nearby convent of a fervent Catholic persuasion, where they pray to the Virgin Mary still — like praying to an atomic warhead! Giant slabs of oak mixed with slices of plane (so full of fresh alcohol it emits a beautiful blue flame) roared in the central chimney of the grand salon; here whole *gigots* peppered with fresh garlic and ginger roasted their way steadily towards the table — the most hospitable in a country celebrated for its hospitality.

At first sight the title of the great commonplace book, *Obs and Inks*, seemed somewhat esoteric, but the reality was less daunting, for the shortened phrase simply stood for the observations and inklings which it was supposed to house. It was intended to indicate the haphazard and spasmodic nature of our corporate thinking about Provence compiled over several winters and springs in the old château. The stout leather-backed volume stood in a fireside nook by the great chimney "where once the agents of the Inquisition had actually roasted heretics alive!" (Aldo). It was always open, spread out upon the broad back of a wooden sculpted eagle with outspread wings, and perched on a cathedral lectern between two priceless candlesticks. It was argued that in between mulling wine or roasting chestnuts we would spare a moment to jot down stray thoughts or other memoranda which at some future date would be sifted and sorted into a quarry for the use of the hypothetical scribe who embarked on the famous book. So far all that had transpired in the nature of documentation was a commentary of bewildering prolixity and variety and no form of order whatsoever (or at least not yet). Moreover it was in various hands, for everyone had been encouraged to contribute his mite, obs or inks. The housebook must once have served as a seventeenth-century farmer's stocktaking book, as it also contained some ancient inventories concerned with the vines of the property. Poetry. Some translations. Dirty limericks (Aldo much admired the sweetness and precision of the form). A small anthology of the jokes which surround the names of Marius and Olive, the famous Provençal cross-talk duo whose backchat is supposed to exemplify the Midi's *esprit*.

No book about the place would be complete without some reference to these two wiseacres, so perhaps this is the place to resurrect one of their famous jokes. One fine day they were shipwrecked and found themselves on a raft in the Indian Ocean, half dead from heat and starvation. Marius after deep reflection said to Olive: "Olive, I have been thinking things over and have reluctantly come to a decision. I cannot stand any more malnutrition. Of what use is little Jules (his member) in a situation like this? None! I am going to cut it off and have it for lunch." Olive showed great concern. "Not so fast, Marius," she said. "Why don't you flatter it a little — there may be enough for two!"

In the past, the adventures of Marius and Olive, duly illustrated, were issued in the form of pedlar's chapbooks and sold at the village fairs and the *fêtes votives* all over Provence.

* * *

Aldo had collected data towards a novel which was to base itself on the imagined private life of Pontius Pilate. According to Aldo, Pilate was the last of the true Romans and the first of the new Europeans — our author, mentor and representative in the Underworld. Sometimes, when drunk, Aldo cast himself in the role of Socrates' "Voice" and indulged in specious and somewhat incoherent arguments between himself and the inquisitorial "Voice":

ALDO: Pilate, I presume!
VOICE: I would have known you anywhere!
ALDO: Except here?
VOICE: Except here, yes. It's in the hands.
ALDO: The eternal washing? I know!

The washing of the hands was followed by the Christian laying-on of the hands in baptism — the slow ruin of the European sensibility from guilt to superstition. Original sin as the aboriginal inheritance of man. Pilate's poor wife foresaw all this with typical female intuition: she warned him to watch out for that little hysteric as he would only bring trouble in the wake of his unhappy monomania. So it proved. When he died, poor Pilate's body was tossed into an empty well in Vienne: another malefic town of which there are many in Provence. A centre of the Black Arts in the alchemical sense. The Templars were at last abolished in Vienne, taking their secret with them. In Aldo's view they were really concealed Lombardy bankers and worked in close harmony with the Cathars. Their financial strength was built upon usury. I am not quite sure how well founded this view is. But certainly they were suffused with feelings of guilt — or how could they

17

have given themselves up so easily, without either reaction or defence? They were, after all, the most powerful Order in the Christendom of the day. To surrender without a blow struck, or a word spoken in their own defence . . . the whole episode smells of sulphur and the black arts!

I was almost ready to be convinced.

By the same token Aldo's favourite philosopher, Demonax, was the one who left us only one aphorism — a riddle, really: "At last a philosopher who knew how to keep his mouth shut, which is the real secret. Demonax! I always imagine that Pontius studied with him before being appointed as governor. Indeed I once wrote a novelized biography of the unfortunate in which I made him study under a philosopher, whose line of inquiry was more Asiatic than Western. Demonax taught in asides, the spontaneous nature of thought was his obsession. He invoked the involuntary! Often his silences lasted for months. He produced ur-thoughts which surfaced purely out of 'right attention.' Pilate learned how to hesitate from him. Too much interest in virtue (the desirable) was to be deplored because it robbed it of spontaneity. Demonax taught him to say, 'I think: therefore I was!' *Je pense donc je suppose.*

"In India he mastered the Dharmic knack of seeing round death; and so through yoga mobilizing the blessed amnesia of the orgasm, making it progressively more and more conscious. With the fall of Rome what was there left to do but preach by silence? Sex has eaten the heart out of time and money has eaten the spirit out of sex. The lustful glory will not last. We are living among bankers who are hunting for a suckling experience, milk of the word, *quoi!* In epochs when love is at risk, art most unhappily is forced to preach.

> *Her liquid assets are her silken sighs*
> *So rubbing noses with her God she dies!"*

– II –

Baptisms

My own baptism as a fully fledged Mediterranean dates from a momentous evening just before the outbreak of the last war, when on a night of full moon I managed to steal up on to the flanks of the Greek Acropolis with my sleeping bag, there to lie in the shadow of the caryatids. A night of windless serene, silent save for the flurrying and mewing of the little owls called the "Scops," once the confidantes of Athena. I was woken at dawn to find myself the object of sympathetic curiosity, for a small flock of sheep was browsing around me in the care of a smiling young shepherd. In those faraway days Athens boasted a couple of flocks of sheep and each day they crossed the city, stopping the traffic as they dawdled across the Syntagma, the Athenian Piccadilly. The young shepherd informed me that he was a priest in the making, and this did not surprise me, for I had already sensed that combined with the luxuriance and efflorescence of Mediterranean culture went (together with the old classical sensuality and romantic reticence) a streak of self-abnegation, of asceticism. Licence and frugality were sisters under the skin — like poetry and mathematics.

Almost a third of a century later I was to wake up in similar fashion, surrounded by sheep, but this time in another context, for I had spent the night asleep in the waterless garrigues around Nîmes, bedded down in my little camping car. The sun was up, and I was under the sardonic scrutiny of another sort of shepherd, one who looked rather like Jehovah, complete with flowing beard and commanding manner. He was curious and friendly, and we shared a ritual *canon* of red wine to salute the dawned day. Jérôme, for it was he, was not really a shepherd, he was filling in time for a few francs; he was my first real tramp, and like his Athenian predecessor was also a priest — but in reverse, for he had taken leave voluntarily of a vocation which, he had discovered, did not really suit him. Provence had brought him to his senses — so he said; and at a single bound he had taken to the road, had joined *La Cloche*, that great brotherhood of scamps and contemplatives and dissenters which, in those days, could be seen everywhere in Provence, marching and counter-marching across the land. One bulging pocket held their litre of red wine while the other was swollen with the newspaper which wrapped their loaf of bread and which, while they lunched, would give them their staple of news about a world they had abandoned.

Jérôme warmly approved of my long association with and attachment to Greece, which he had never seen — "except here," he added, and then went on to say, "You won't be far from it here, though at first the predominance of Roman monuments will seem quite overwhelming. After all, there are more vestiges of Rome in Provence than there are in the peninsula itself! You can't escape it!"

Jérôme was from Paris, an intellectual on the run, and I came to count on his rare visits to my little *mazet*, for his conversation was full of insight and his knowledge of the place almost encyclopaedic. With him I made a couple of long three-day jaunts across the country to enrich my impressions. If you want to know how long the Roman mile can be or how the legionary felt on a long march in midsummer, or in winter with the Mistral up, you should take up with a tramp! But — not any tramp will do . . . and it became clear that Jérôme was no ordinary tramp.

Over the years I have met quite a number of his fellows: when first I arrived in Provence they were numerous and very much in evidence and indeed were made very welcome by the Provençaux. They always turned out to be renegade house-painters or seamen or agricultural workers driven by drink or mental trouble to become vagabonds — to succumb to the malady with the delightful name of "dromomania" . . . I suppose they contained as a profession the statutory number of drunks and eccentrics and perhaps even criminal vagabonds capable of giving the police headaches. But *La Cloche* enjoyed a sort of envious creative respect, as if the general public felt that these whiskered gentlemen were really at heart peripatetic philosophers who had opted out of ordinary society in order to make an almost religious retreat, perhaps to "redefine their deaths" while there was yet time. Secretly everyone felt that to take to the road was an act of romantic glory and philosophic insight — and this may be correct. I remembered from my childhood in India something of the same attitude towards the *sadhu* or holy man who had taken to the jungle in search of a verifiable truth, with the desire to rediscover submission as a fine art and help it to become a corporate philosophy. Certainly when I first met Jérôme he was sailing under these colours and enjoyed wide respect as a lettered man. He had many friends in the villages he frequented, friends of every colour who, like him, might do a day or two of carpentry or house-painting to make ends meet. But they were at heart solitaries. One of them lived in a tub in Avignon, and slept on straw like Diogenes. He had a commonplace book in which he preserved stray thoughts and philosophic jottings, which did not lack originality.

But the avocation seems to be under stress. The whole character of *La Cloche* has been changed by the new motorways which criss-cross the country. The tramps have retreated into small defensive colonies in the more unsavoury quarters of Toulon and Marseille, just as the gypsy life has started to become stabilized in fixed places where the children can attend school: their caravans now have television sets mounted. City culture is here to stay, presumably.

Punks at the Parthenon

We have never loved anyone
Or believed in anything wise:
And for some time now
Have come to believe we are
A variety of mutinous angel
Candid and absolute in our nothingness.
Goaded by soft unreason to despise
The tumble-dried life of modern love.
"As above, so below," says the prophet.
"An ego poached in salt . . . means WOE.*"*
An acropolis of broken teeth beckons.
Yet three of such kisses and you are hooked
As we say in heroin lingo, hooked!
Between conniving thighs an addict lies.
To lead you by syringefuls to the land of sighs.

A journey with Jérôme was doubly interesting, because his accent gave him away as a man of the north and he was good-humouredly chaffed for "speaking pointed" (*parler pointu*) which is Provence's way of showing distaste for the Paris accent. I suppose a good translation of the phrase would be something like "talking posh!" I myself, as a real foreigner, would be beyond criticism however I chose to speak — the sacred law of hospitality looked after that. It was amusing to feel more at home than a native-born Frenchman, for the broad-vowelled Provençal on his home ground will try to convince you that he lives in a subtle disharmony with the northerners who "speak pointed," and who patronize the lazy moribund operatic Midi which is the image projected by the music hall and the visiting journalists and writers. It is not entirely true, though some of the findings of Pagnol are near enough the bone, and the story-book personages, like the immortal Marius and Olive, do represent the very spirit of Marseille. Yet it was a pointer to the disharmony which has always reigned not simply between north and south but between a Mediterranean culture and the rest of the world. The difference is not wider than the gulf which separates Irish, Scots and Welsh in the realm of regional character and mental attitude. The lands where the vine and the olive flourish insist on a particularity which is embodied by the men and women who inhabit them for any length of time. (The Rhône boatmen until recently called one bank of the river "Empire" and the other "Kingdom" to stress a difference of attitude.) And though Provence has been united to France for 400 years or so, there is no part of France which has kept its individuality like the Midi. Indeed, as historians tell us, there was a time when it was touch and go whether she herself might not absorb the lands of the Capets and of Valois — thus swallowing France rather than being swallowed by her!

Caesar, whose crafty insight was equal to most of the problems of history and politics, divided Gaul into three parts; later historians reduced the number to two. Drawing a girdle around her, they established a dichotomy of language: the north of the *langue d'oil* and the south of the *langue d'oc*. Above the human girdle are the head and the heart, below, the digestive and the sexual apparatus — a fair analogy between the human organism and the French geography. The character of the north is aware, deliberate and analytical, the cool mechanical forebrain at work. Paris, you might say, is the heart. Head and heart reign over the whole body. It is a conscious control. But the subconscious is operative in the belly and the loins; south of our imaginary girdle, sense and sensibility, untroubled by excess of logic and ratiocination, develop the riches and warmth for the whole system. The north supplies ideas and motives, the south, feeling and emotion, to combine in a rich spiritual mix which can best be studied in those sunwarmed provinces far from the capital. The broad-spoken meridionals are more natural and easygoing than the men of the north, more given to poetry and music, not to mention rhetoric and debate, than their northern compatriots. Formulations, classification, inventories — they rapidly weary of such data and are renowned for lack of method. Among the great men born to France one can so often discern a pattern of talents: for scientists, philosophers and thinkers tend to be of northern stock, while the poets, artists and men of action come from the Mediterranean southern fringes.

But I could see from the look of impatience on Jérôme's face that I was wearying him with my laborious evaluations, for every statement can, indeed must, be qualified a hundred ways if it is to resemble even provisional truth, and if geography stands for anything, the variety of soils, airs, and water in France should preclude generalization. How to compress into a single entity something as various as the slag heaps of the Ardennes, Norman orchards, the rolling wheat of the Beauce lands, the lofty Cévennes . . . not to mention monstrous provincial suburbs around Crusader towns, serene châteaux, tiny explicit mediaeval churchyards, or fishy blue-eyed Mediterranean ports? How to splice up the intuitional impact of vine cross-stitching in the Midi in winter, rice-green in spring, claret and hock in hue in autumn with leaves like lemon wedges floating in China tea?

*   *   *

What are the French really like? While Jérôme grumbled on, I found myself thinking back to my own early youth, to the first shock of my encounter — at about twenty years of age — with Paris. It was like a sudden unpremeditated chord on the piano — a chord I had never struck before. The city was full of a subtle sort of oxygen which mounted to the head. I realized I was among people who valued pleasure as a religious and aesthetic good, as soul-food! At every turn I was shocked and instructed, as much by the light as the wine. Moreover, while walking in the Luxembourg Gardens I had been adopted by a young and pretty French student who had decided to take my education in hand — not only in the matter of love, though this was paramount for someone brought up in England — but also in the matter of food. In her little attic under the eaves she composed a memorable *croque-monsieur* the like of which I had never tasted before, with a sureness of touch . . . It was magic, and it answered to the red wine like an echo in a sea-shell. Nothing like this could ever have happened to me in London where the girls were all descended from Canute. But even this marking experience was not all. In my conversations with Gabrielle I saw a temperament at work which, I suddenly realized, rendered the French as different from ourselves as, say, the Japanese. This young woman not only had sensitized taste buds, she was also a *fervente* of paint: we had stopped before an oil painting and she had talked with a wonderful simplicity about her passion for the water-colours of Almendro, adding nonchalantly: "I am buying one on the instalment plan — just made the first downpayment — phew! it's expensive; but with the next I take possession — do you realize what that means? I shall have it here over my bed!" She had in fact started her collection of personal paintings though she had barely turned twenty! I was in a ferment of shame and astonishment as I lay beside her on the uncomfortable cot in which she slept, and helped her with her *devoir*. "Are we French so different, after all?" she asked, and I told her of my delight to find a large notice reading *Défense d'uriner* on the Chambre des Députés. So they were anarchists to boot? No wonder the artists of the whole world felt at home in France. My surprise surprised her. What, she wanted to know, did we have written up outside the Mother of Parliaments . . . ?

Neither in the matter of food nor of art were we the slightest bit similar to the French. I saw an article in the newspaper which informed me that in Paris alone there were over 6,000 Sunday painters from every walk of life just daubing away for the pure aesthetic pleasure of the game! And if you reside in the country for any length of time you soon realize that every inch of unused garage and loft space in the French home is taken up with finished and unsold paintings, waiting for wall space. What is so encouraging is that the proclivity is really a popular one — it is the people who paint, not only the artists; the artisans who spent a summer tidying up the ruins of my cottage in the waterless garrigues north of Nîmes were all awake to the pleasure of paint even though they themselves were not executants. I had always thought of art and high cuisine as being part of the privileges which belonged to riches. These humble masons of Nîmes had a blowout every weekend with their families, each time in a different restaurant, and they boasted that the other artisans of the city were just like them. They ate like sportsmen, and if the restaurants were no good or too expensive — why, they could put them out of business at the snap of a finger! It was a heartening surprise to feel that the quality of bread and wine and food were not fads which were kept up for the snobbish and the rich, but the result of a whole people's demand. In this sense my own people remained relatively philistine, it seemed to me. For us *Grande Cuisine* and fine wine were "upper-class." Not so here.

Food as one of the fine arts, then, is not just the domain

of the rich. I recall another small incident which struck me. In the middle of winter at the small hotel near the Fontaine de Vaucluse I arrived somewhat late for dinner. The only other diners were two garage mechanics from Avignon with their wives or sisters — I could not make out which. But the little hotel was an expensive one and known for its rare cuisine. Indeed, when I entered the manageress was busy trying to persuade them to taste the last four portions of venison which remained on her menu. It was such a treat, she pleaded, and such a rare delicacy that they might never come across it again. Why not try it? The enthusiasm of her clients was obvious, but they were not very well off, and hesitatingly they asked the price of the portions. They then turned out their pockets and counted out their money scrupulously before deciding in favour of the adventure — for that was the correct word for it. It was an aesthetic adventure and it also involved a suitable wine. The whole thing was most carefully costed out, and their sober appreciation of the dish was quite professional. Yet they must have been in their early twenties, the four of them, and people of modest station. I could not help mentally setting in their place two English garage mechanics with their wives . . . A contrast of attitudes which would reveal a good deal about national ethos!

Another example: when Bernard Miche took over the abandoned carpet factory in Sommières and decided to build it into a restaurant, he could hardly cook. But with diligence and study he turned himself into a great chef. At the very beginning, when he was still green, he told me that he was only employing people who were serious about food as a career, and that he, together with his collaborators — two youths of sixteen and eighteen, and an under-chef — had agreed to establish a *cagnotte* (a "kitty") with the intention, when it was full, to take the car up to Lyon and spend a couple of days tasting the masterpieces of the great chef Pombal, and learning from him the secrets of high cuisine.

It was as if they were going to consult the high priest, and the entire team was united in its ardour, its fervour. When they came back they talked with reverence of the whole visit, as if they had been to see the Pope! They had actually been initiated, if that is not too strong a word, by the few words of counsel which the Master had let fall. They had learned finally that recipes were available to all and there were no secrets; but each master had his own style and each marked the recipe with his own character and emphasis, his personal touch. In the case of Pombal it was only a question of time — he had extended the cooking time of his dishes, and lowered the speed of *cuisson*, explaining, "They are more imbued with my spirit than dishes which are rushed. Time is the key." Bernard had at once started to meditate on this factor and change his own rate of cooking. One little word had changed everything.

But here we are in the domain of art, of creation. I am reminded of the mystic who, after thirty years of study and self-torture, finally mastered the art of levitation. He went to thank his guru for the success. The old sage congratulated him warmly on the victory and said, "It is wonderful news and I commend you most warmly. But now, tell me one further thing. Can you refrain?" Just a few words — but they throw a shaft of light from a superior soul, a superior vision, and irradiate the whole field of one's endeavour.

The secret of the French attitude is simply that cooking is included among the fine arts and accorded the same respect as a gift for painting. But the pleasure and enrichment for an artist living in France is the feeling that the whole population is subtly engaged in the same debate with itself — namely, how to turn living into something more than just existing.

Once, while waiting for someone in a café in Nîmes, I scribbled some accounts on the back of the bill. When the time came to leave, I duly paid the waiter who, without thinking, tore up the check. When he caught sight of my scribblings on the nether side he turned pale. "*Quelle horreur,*" he cried. "*J'ai détruit vos brouillons, Monsieur!*" I thought he was going to fall at my feet and clasp them in an agony of remorse. "How awful! I have destroyed your rough-notes!" It was obvious that I had been roughing out a poem on the bill, and he had inadvertently destroyed it!

The point is worth stressing, for it is one of the keys to the French point of view, to the Gallic character, one of the deepest points of difference with us, the Anglo-Saxons. Nowhere is there a more acute and vivid illustration of this basic difference than in the writings of Stendhal, in the marvellous description of his meeting with his adored Byron, a meeting so much longed for and on which he had set great store. As an artist of roughly the same magnitude he knew the importance of Byron, the size of his spiritual image, so to speak. Yet everything went wrong. Byron behaved clumsily, with overwhelming conceit and condescension, and the French writer was upset and wounded. Yet in trying to look beyond his personal chagrin and analyse the reasons, he finally concluded that the Englishman appeared to be more interested in being a Lord than in being a great Poet. The snob and the dandy seemed to rule his heart, not the supreme poet whom Stendhal so much admired. How different the French attitude — for a Poet was almost holy in conception, while to be a Lord was romantic and delightful and helped with the fair sex, but it didn't go very deep. The same holds good in France today — the word Art weighs heavily in the scales. It will even help with a difficult *douanier* or immigration official which — heaven knows! — renders France different from any other country I have ever known.

*   *   *

And Provence? Jérôme: "Even Provence has never completely and wholly existed in a single form. The Roman Provincia has expanded and retracted in space throughout history.

Indeed, it is more an idea than a place. You will find this out quite soon."

Provence was not really a place! It is not really a separate entity with boundaries and a separated, self-realized soul as, say, Switzerland is. It is a beautiful metaphor born of Caesar's impatience with a geographical corridor stacked with the ruins of a hundred cultures, a hundred nations and tribes, a hundred armies. The capricious rivers which scribbled over its surface often flooded and inhibited the free movement of regiments and of trade caravans alike. The Roman roads when they came did much to render the place coherent, and to clarify the prevailing doctrine and predisposition of the country's inner being, its true soul which could be summed up by the word dissent. It is bold, of course, to use such phrases, for one runs the danger of being thought to be fantasizing, but even a brief residence here will convince that if much of the historical side of Provence often seems paradoxical, it is because of the overlay of different cultures which are all slowly conforming to the genius of the place, but at different speeds. The most powerful and the most consistent, like the Roman, have left more relics through which we can decipher their life-style. But it is only overlay, for under them we find Saracen and Greek relics, while even the modern shepherds offer us Stone Age echoes in their habits. It is what has remained obstinately constant and apparently ineradicable that strikes you as time goes by. The long roots stretch back into Greek and Roman history, and of course through these great channels into the Mediterranean world as a cultural epic form — a masterpiece of realized memory. It is more emblematic than metaphoric, more poetry than prose! And in the heart of its historic change lies a continuity and consistence which shows the pious strength of these hills and rivers to bend man and shape him into an original thought-form — the place expressing itself through his body and mind as surely as a sculptor expresses himself in the clay he works or the stone he carves. One can believe in Caesar and Mistral as spiritual coevals, and in the whole tapestry of its tempestuous history as all being appropriate, all belonging right here and nowhere else.

From the purely historical point of view, what seems remarkable is the long tally of violence and drama which characterizes this land of green glades and noble forests, a minor paradise if ever there was one. Yet Goths, Franks, Vandals, Saracens, every variety of invader seems to have subjected it to the extremes of pillage, destruction, naked war. It was as if its beauty was too much for them, they went berserk. They trampled underfoot what they could not bear. One thinks of Charles Martel in the eighth century filling the Nîmes arenas with wood and setting them alight in the vain hope of burning this great Roman trophy to the ground — in vain, happily, but the marks of his fires are still to be seen today. What on earth could have possessed him to order such a thing, so base in its utter senselessness? Yet he is not the only one: others did worse things.

One thinks at once of the proud enumeration of Roman buildings of Provence in the great poem of Mistral, his "Calendau"; yet the poet only mentions the surviving Roman arches of Orange, Carpentras, Cavaillon, St-Rémy and St-Chamas, before turning his attention to the huge aqueduct bridge we call the Pont du Gard, certainly the most picturesque of monuments, and the crown of the Roman experience in this honeyed land. He overlooks, however, those others destroyed by man, like the three arches of Arles, the admirable arch, that of Constantine, and lastly the arch destroyed as recently as 1839 . . . When one reflects on the number of Roman theatres, monuments, temples and arches which are still to be seen in Provence today, one realizes how thoroughly the whole province must have been Romanized. No wonder Mistral himself, feeling this historic link, could boast in another poem that the men of Provence were "Gallo-Romans and gentlemen!" In contrast to many other invaders, Rome came, and came with every intention of staying. You could not start work on a monument like one of these unless you felt certain of at least half a century of peace ahead of you. Time for such people must have been dense with the calm certainty of a rich futurity ahead, whatever the forebodings caused by the vandals hanging about the outer gates of the Empire. Time to block-build in these huge nuggets of stone, raised into the sky without pulleys and jointed so deftly and in such sure phase that mortar was superfluous. The sheer size and weight of this sort of building is cowing, for after all these huge edifices are popular and demotic in intent, not religious, funerary or monumental. The aqueducts ferried water to the cities, the arenas were places of entertainment and not worship. They faithfully conveyed to the public the philosophy of bread and circuses which kept them civilized and obedient to those who ruled them. No, Caesar was not cynical, for it was a fair estimate of the limitations and the powers of the ordinary voting man. It is true of ourselves today; the same welter of anarchic impulses, of violent sub-conscious yearnings are now soothed by the erotic violence of the cinema — murder's secret surrogate and alibi!

Once, and once only, I managed to persuade my friend Jérôme to submit to the degradation of motor-travel — it was to visit La Turbie, that strange jumbled monument which marks the border of Roman Gaul. It is perched on a small acropolis and is not a great distance from Monte Carlo. Needless to say, all the hopelessly civilized and sophisticated coastal reaches of the Côte d'Azur were anathema to him. It resembled too closely the civilization he was trying to get away from; he preferred to lurk about in the landscapes of the more backward and undeveloped corners of the Vaucluse and the Gard, and I do not, did not, blame him. Yet we spent an hour or two in the wind and rain on that dramatic pro-montory, prowling about the remains of one of the most impressive monuments of antiquity, raised in honour of Augustus in about 6 BC and perched strategically in scenographic splendour on a high spur of the Via Julia Augusta, the coastal road which was declared open in 12 BC after the long-awaited pacification of the Alps. They had fought hard for it in a long series of deliberate battles and were fully aware that the final one vindicated all the preceding ones (25, 16, 15, 14 BC) with their bitter losses in men and equipment. The magnitude as well as the site of the trophy expressed Rome's pride in the whole adventure, and the golden letters of the sculpted citation enumerated the forty-four vanquished peoples, and stressed that the land-mass now pacified stretched between the Superior and Inferior Seas (the Adriatic and the Tyrrhenian). And the movement of goods and minerals and other precious items up and down the Rhône linked Rome with Paris and the Channel. The great trophy of La Turbie celebrates this link and despite its smashed and muddled state it remains impressive and moving. Or so I found it. And in what concerns Provence we should accustom ourselves to the notion that it is, after all, a part of France despite its Mediterranean heart and quixotic manners. How did all this come about?

The rivers of the world achieved it, for they provided a pathway, a moving carpet for mariners, explorers and traders, a whole transport system for exports and imports. In secure and propitious corners, counters were founded to house goods for barter — Marseille began thus. Indeed the history of France could be written around its rivers both northern and southern, not to speak of the great cities which sprang up on the estuaries they formed wherever they touched the sea. The key to Provence in this sense is the Rhône — a poet's river if ever there was one — and I am not thinking only of Mistral, the Provençal Dante, whose historic and linguistic importance makes him the foremost literary representative of the Provençal ethos — somewhat like Tagore is for the Indian.

(It is no accident that both poets became Nobel prizewinners, as much for what they represented as for what they actually wrote.)

The way was now open for further Roman expansion towards the north, towards Europe. The statue of the victorious Augustus watched over it from the top of a terminal pyramid, while parts of the jumbled masonry which litters the site have even suggested to some that perhaps there was a pharos atop the whole complex. But the monument is in a sad mess today for the shattered fragments have been spliced together anyhow and all coherence is lost. Here one finds a captive in chains, and there a warrior with raised sword, or a helmet enlaced with garlands near a belted tunic and sword . . .

The tribes in question have also vanished, melted into the mists of history. Yet the land remains with all its beauties and its reticences. My bearded companion expressed no such sentiments and seemed to be deeply distressed by the proximity of the playgrounds of Nice and Monte Carlo. Yes, but Jérôme was in the toils of that most inflexible of serpents, memory, and his fuliginous eye roved over the sun-dappled Alpilles with an incurable nostalgia, as if questing the shadow of that youthful self who long ago decided on an impulse to throw up Paris and all it stood for, and to go south into the Midi using a second-hand bicycle . . . All change is for the worse, his attitude seemed to say, and while I have no cause to disagree with the thought, it renders life a little more livable if one can find place for a more indulgent view of the contemporary.

If Jérôme had one fixed point from which to judge the whole subject of Provence (which, despite the abandoned book, is ever-present, always on the boil) it is the oft-invoked *pérennité des choses*, the feeling that all history is endlessly repeating itself, perpetuating itself, not in the form of a chronological ribbon, a linear form, but in a momentous simultaneousness. The form may change but the content hardly seems to vary. This was an article of faith which allowed him to view the whole history of the land as a sort of shadow-play dictated by the fact that Provence is simply a corridor down which, or up which, people have rushed bound for other landfalls. Yes, but underneath it all the place has a spirit of its own which starts to modify the invader if only he will stay long enough, starts to model his sensibility, invest him with its own secret lore.

– III –

Terre d'élection de la haute magie

They had been drinking a good deal. Aldo stood up and said: "I wish to announce the possibility of a tremendous happiness — total bliss in fact, as a norm within the reach of everyone rich or poor! The state is attainable with practice and concern, and is conditioned by our attitude to death, and in consequence to nature as a whole, including our own. Hurrah, so to speak!" Then he fell down and dropped off to sleep.

"Suggested title for autobiography:
I was Nero's governess.
Cultivate that cannibal glide
Face closed up with
Mouth like a zipper
Time zipping tide like
the breakfast kipper.

"She served the children beignets
Of precious little human ears
Deep-fried in batter
Baby fruit, what better?
The unction of tiny tongues
Snails like foreskins on holiday. Gastronomy Royal!
Hail Human Snail!"

Aldo pinned notes from his reading to a pier-glass which kept up a wobbly concubinage with the fireplace with its burning oak and plane. All the points marked *nota bene* as if of the greatest importance — perhaps they were. Such as: "The resined wine we now call *retsina*, and think of as Greek, is mentioned in Martial's Epigrams — a Roman invention." Other notes, more nebulous, such as: "Once you have read Propertius, you understand that words like 'bungalow' or 'torpedo' or 'waterfall' can give a true poet an erection."

"Superficially, the Principle of Indeterminacy may appear to rub noses with the Tao or the Supreme Intuition as exemplified in the Dharma experience, BUT . . . a radical difference of intention separates them. The fruit of Jewish monotheism was the scientific rationalism which afflicts us, for the Jewish intention was to exploit matter by smashing it anatomically and extracting its marketable energy to yield gold! The philosophic curiosity was not pure and disinterested, something which might provide new clues to self-realization within the pure inherence of the universe. The first attitude seeks to exploit, the second solicits the power contained in the passive style, an art of surrender. The hunt for a better knack than at present exists! How to come to terms with the involuntary crisis of Light."

We are in the realm of magic, of course.

I am reminded of the first winter I spent in Provence as a guest of Aldo, a winter of deep snow and heaped fires of oak and olive. It was to "farce the goose," according to his invitation; and this operation was something worth watching because of the dexterity with which he handled the *bistouri*. One had forgotten that Aldo had done a stint in a medical school and should know how to handle a scalpel. But in order to farce his goose he first had to spreadeagle it and then bone it *per anum*, and this was a job of the greatest delicacy, a real medical operation, specially when the goose was a large one; it usually took about an hour, during which we sat around

by the fire giving him futile advice and slowly gathering together the materials for the farce, of which the principal in-
gredients, if I remember, were ginger and fennel, laced with
cinnamon and saffron!

It was one evening during these exchanges that the subject
of magic came up. "Like you, I was at first disposed to take
the matter lightly — I thought it a sort of journalist's *boutade*
when I saw the headline 'Provence: *terre de la haute magie*' over
an article which insisted that since Roman times and even
before, black magic and alchemy had flourished underground
here. But if you read your daily paper while you are in Provence, you will be struck by the number of soothsayers, magicians, palmists, astrologers and *voyantes* generally who
advertise there. Also the variety, for half Africa is represented
by known practitioners of the divinatory arts." The bones of
his goose crunched agreeably in the jaws of his beautiful
retriever, while his friend Marmouze, the little police doctor,
lent a hand with the preparing of the farce, reminding us the
while that the original Cabala was hatched at Vauvert. As a
police surgeon who spent most of his night on urgency calls
he had many piquant things to tell us about this type of
experience.

"If you are at all sensitive to the emanations of place you
will at once find yourself reacting to a town like Nîmes, which
was once as famous as Eleusis, a magical centre and spa.
Every time you call a plumber in to repair a pipe, he digs out
of the ground a hundred little ex-votos in terracotta or metal
or stone. There are whole drifts of these propitiatory offerings
knocking about, just as under Byzance the ikons litter the
chapels with scribbled prayers on rotting parchments . . .
Myself, I don't doubt that much is still going on: every time
this year when I was in a police sweep for drugs like cocaine
or heroin we ran into other things which more or less hinted
as much. An example is the fragments of Egyptian mum-

mies — *mummia* it is still called. It is widely used in casting spells and provoking visionary states! Yes, still today! There are still tomb-robbers who make a living by robbing Egyptian tombs in the sand dunes around Cairo to provide the *mummia* which comes into Provence through places like Sfax and Carthage and Algiers. It comes in fattish wafers which can be passed off as dried fish — a comestible the Indians serve with curry, though that is real fish you crumble on the dish, whereas this is a slice of dried body! It cockered up the vatic side of the patient, or perhaps his sexual powers. In the museums with their private collections based on Nîmes you see how often the phallus was the votive object offered up to the shrine: the cult of Priapus was a flourishing one, and Nîmes was renowned as a centre of medical practices and magical cults!"

And then, while the fire was being heaped with wood, Marmouze cried, "And what about your baby? Have you told him about your golden baby?" Aldo had not; so taking a brief rest from his surgical labours (entrusting the scalpel to the little doctor), he dived into a side-chapel and from a violin-case on a mantelpiece produced a pleasant golden baby, a sort of sleeping *putto*, thrusting it unceremoniously into my hands. It gave off a dark poetic glow and was very light — I thought it might be a model in plaster which had been gilded. It suggested at first a carnival decoration. But seeing my doubtful look he reassured me that it was indeed a real baby: "Embalmed and gilded by these very hands! I have had several serious offers for her as an instrument of carnal magic, but I only once entertained the idea. I took fright at the result and since then have kept her here."

"What happened?"

But he wouldn't tell me. Only that "it happened at Queribus on the old stone gallows which are still in place there, in a tower open to the sky. The eyes were picked out by eagles.

I had to replace them when I gilded her. It gives her that strange look like Mary Queen of Scots (but she, poor dear, was never down here, I think)."

He proceeded to tell me its history. Towards the end of his medical studies he had fallen in with a gypsy at the yearly fête at the Saintes Maries de la Mer. He seemed rather an unusual type. His little caravan came from Carthage, and they were smugglers of objects robbed from tombs, headstones, carvings, votive insignia, etc. As if to give verisimilitude to his story, Aldo thrust a dried human finger into my other hand. It was this gypsy who had asked the medical student if he knew how to embalm and, if so, would he exercise his art on a "real" corpse . . .

"I had always had a morbid interest in the subject of embalming; indeed I had chosen it as the subject of my thesis — it had given me an excuse to travel a bit in the Orient to examine specimens in museums like Cairo and Istanbul. The practice is delicate, but not really complicated — not like this boned goose which Marmouze is making a mess of . . . But it was on a mediaeval mummy that I first saw how handsome a gilded corpse can be. Naturally at that time I simply thought that my gypsy wanted to sell it as a gruesome little curiosity for amateurs of the genre, until he told me that there was a brisk market for such things in Africa among witch-doctors and magicians of every grade. They used them to cast spells. They even figured in inter-tribal affairs if they had a strong emanation, strong *ju ju* or *mana*! I was just starting work in a crowded public obstetrical ward where the odd dead baby could be popped into a briefcase and carried off with nobody the wiser and no questions asked. I set up a tin bath and the tools of my new trade in the garage — a good surgeon favours perfect seclusion! And for a while I pursued my avocation with nothing to hinder me. Even the professional undertakers used to turn a blind eye towards me since my little thefts were not too flagrant nor too frequent. And even though I suspected my gypsy of cheating me royally, the price we were paid for each baby was handsome indeed, and while my production was limited the articles were so choice that they sold like hot cakes! I was even able to meet with some exceptional orders, like a necklace of human fingers or a dried skull for a cabalist of Arles. (Emptying the brain case presents some problems!)

"But in general I met with no obstacles until one day I was denounced by a mother suffering from puerperal fever, and her complaints were backed up by an undertaker who was jealous of the money I was making. It was catastrophic. There was a note in the local paper hinting at grave robbery and the desecration of tombs and I found myself in court. The gypsy was picked up on some other similar charge and sentenced to several years in gaol. I escaped, but with a crippling fine and what amounted to a warning against my activities. So here I am, once more a pauper, and surgically limited to a Christmas goose; although recently I have had offers of an embalming project of some importance which might restore my fortunes once and for all. I am wondering whether to accept these tempting later offers or not. If caught, I could get a prison sentence which would be a bore. But the gains would be considerable. She is of exceptional beauty, the dead girl. Daughter of the old count you met here last Christmas, do you recall?"

Indeed I did. Chief among Aldo's friends of that epoch, an old and somewhat impoverished Roman Papal Count, Reynaldo de Saturnin was not the only one of his special breed, though in the region he counted as such — a *rara avis*. His scholarship was as unexceptionable as his humour was both sly and his wit dry. Usually the *grand seigneur* in Provence is more of a rough diamond, an activist of field and stream and worshipper of horseflesh and the taurine arts, whereas our Reynaldo lived a somewhat sleepy and bookish life in his château outside Arles with only one servant to cater to his needs. His wife had died some years before and he lived with an only daughter of great beauty who, despite the fact that she was a musician of distinction, was deaf and dumb. She spent her life reading and editing scores — the château library boasted a notable collection of music purchased by him on his numerous voyages abroad.

It was pure chance that during a hard winter spell the Count found himself on Aldo's doorstep. (Although many years previously they had both spent a period as scholars at the august university of Montpellier, they had lost touch.) The swollen Rhône had jumped its banks and bounds and threadbare bridges. The very noise turned one pale with apprehension. The Count's child had fallen ill and there was not a local doctor to be found during the holiday week of Christmas. Somebody suggested Aldo, although he was not still in active practice, and the Count drove over in his old-fashioned coach, despite the snowy weather, and rapped on the front door with the great brass knocker shaped in the form of a human skull. Hesitant as he was, Aldo allowed himself to be charmed by the concern of the old man; and it was not long before he took a place in the coach and set off to visit the girl. "He talked all the time in a low distracted tone and in a haphazard manner. A servant let us in and I found myself examining a young woman of quite particular magnificence. The only light came from a tall many-branched candelabra which lit up her fairness with a fitful and sulky stare. Her weary blue eyes were set off by the opalescent beauty of her skin, the fever had coloured her cheeks with its touches of rose. She showed signs of some wasting type of malady — perhaps advanced leukaemia? Her weakness and persistent fevers suggested something like that. I told him that I feared that her illness was a progressive one with a terminal issue which was not optimistic. He showed great alarm: indeed he fainted and had a small convulsion of anxiety upon the sofa, under my very eyes, his skin manifesting the quality of porcelain or veined marble. They had a strange beauty, the two of them, and they accepted the glass of whisky I suggested (*en attendant mieux*) with gratitude.

"It was the beginning of a long friendship, and a firm one despite the many intermissions. It was now that I was told that Count Reynaldo was rumoured to have made a study of the black arts, notably the Cabal and the writings of Nostradamus. They even said that he had called the gypsies to help with the illness of his daughter. All in vain, however. By pure sympathy I found myself acting as the family doctor and though I visited the château frequently there was little I could do and I did not disguise the fact. Her infirmity was gaining on us, and the next summer, after a brief crisis, to his great grief and despair she died in his arms. Count Reynaldo was distraught. For a while our whole summer routine — we were supposed to be on holiday — was thrown into anxiety and confusion. She lay there with a kind of exhausted serenity in a saffron robe in a pine coffin embowered with flowers while the burial arrangements were discussed; we ate in silence in the old dining hall by the keep while only Topaze, the Negro chauffeur, was encouraged to play the great concert grand in her honour. Reynaldo sat over his wine, deep in thought.

"Unfortunately there is no medical cure for the pains of bereavement, unless it be drugs or alcohol, but neither really assuages the central wound, the hopeless sense of futile loss. For a while the Count's despair persuaded him to lock himself in and avoid the world, though he kept in touch with me by telephone. But he disappeared from the scene and I supposed that the girl had been duly interred in the family vault which lay on the outskirts of the great mediaeval cemetery, the Alyscamps. The Count's town house had numerous dependencies, among them a handsome group of beehive tombs of Saracen provenance, and it was in one of these that I at last discovered the tomb of his daughter. The tomb itself was

grandiose and had evidently done duty as a chapel, both
Christian and pagan, at different epochs. The central beehive
of the group made a handsome stone sepulchre in which she
lay in state surrounded by waxen fruit and flowers, and lit
by lantern-light and candles. Two old Arlésiennes with da-
mascened shawls sat by her, knitting. With her classical pallor
she looked like some expensive musical instrument in its
case — the trembling of the candles gave an occasional fugitive illusion of life to the whole *nature morte*. The masons
had graven their mortuary inscription and a pile of spades
and trowels and lanterns attested to the recentness of their
visit.

"He had transformed the central chapel into a great refrig-
erator, lining the walls with insulated metal tiles and fasten-
ings to enable him to keep a stable temperature in the tomb.
The two old women, knitting away like the Fates, shivered
with the cold, and so did the Count himself. He had realized
that the present state of things could not last — that he must
devise something less vulnerable than this stony ice-box in
order to house his daughter's body safely. The problem, as
always since the early Middle Ages, had been the presence
of tomb robbers who were always to be found hanging about
the Alyscamps, ready to pounce on a deserted grave or crypt
and carry off what they could find. Nor did their depredations
stop with the spoliation of the burial. It was widely accepted
that the bodies themselves were not safe from physical desecration; one was advised to let them reach an advanced stage
of decomposition before consigning them to the tomb where
the impious hands of the tomb thieves could reach them.
Naturally such thoughts and fears filled the Count with horror and anxiety. Sooner or later the old women would give
up their vigil, despite the pay, and return to their respective
villages. 'There is only one thing to do,' he said, 'I suddenly
realized last night. Embalm her, then I could keep her at the
château in a glass case.' "

At this moment the chimney caught fire and some of the elements of the approaching farce almost followed suit — the diversion made Aldo lose the thread of his discourse in favour of a dissertation on how to bone a goose or a swan from the anus. He enumerated the bones in a pedantic show of medical Latin before authorizing us to go ahead and pour in the farce which had had its due share of attention in an iron colander. In it went now in a steady colourful stream — the nuts, spices, the brown rice and the oriental condiments — before advancing the long mediaeval spit with its spike and rotary drum-roaster which wound itself up like a clock . . .

Sleepwalkers

One rapidly cooling corpse ago
He heard his mother's angel go
On tiptoe in memorial guise,
Finger on lip, smiling and wise,
Finger on heart, thoughtful and slow,
She sank the knife home to the hilt:
He felt the polar stab of guilt.
This was her way of saying No.
The treason was too much to bear
In his heart's core. Ah! Woe!
It slept gothic-nefast and sure
Kiss of some old Slavonic whore.
"Eh bien," he thought, "Je suis bien servi
For daring to believe us free";
When Adam toiled and Eve span
Who was then the gentleman?

– IV –

Bull-worship

Winter can be long and desolate or short and brutal in this inconstant and variable climate; when the snows set in on Mont Ste-Victoire or Mont Aigoual it can drag on like the end of the world. But finally things begin to clear, the river-beds to expel their ice, and the world seems to turn its sleeping cheek towards an invisible but beckoning spring. But the real chronological mark which records it comes with the Pentecostal fires of June, the prolonged holiday with its famous Feria which brings the bull-mania of the extreme south to Arles and Nîmes. The *corridas* cater for both sorts of bullfight, the Spanish and the French, while opera, classical music and jazz are all honoured in the settings they deserve — the giant golden arenas of Nîmes and Arles. It is a real spring rite on pagan lines, this first formal acknowledgement to spring, still today a wonderful prolonged orgy of festal music and drama and games, for all Paris comes down to be present for the early sunlight of the year — either as spectator or performer. Moreover, all Spain puts in an appearance too: for some weeks now the southern roads are full of lorries bringing up the huge Iberian bulls for the sacrificial *corrida*, and bull-magic, bull-worship, is in the air. Arles is full of gypsies, Nîmes full of guitar-playing ensembles of various persuasions and prove-

46

nances — Africa, Hawaii, Réunion, Brooklyn, Polynesia . . . And everything lasts all night through! Music and blood strike a chord which somehow embodies the first cherries and apricots, and the villages fill up with swarthy visitors — casual labour for the harvests as yet to be gathered: asparagus, medlars, mulberries. Not to mention poets, even American poets: critics of civilization whose Michelangelo is Andy Warhol. Never mind, the fiesta is Roman in its comprehensiveness and admits all conditions of men.

> *Limpid is as limpid seems,*
> *Our confusions are in dreams!*

Not least the transcendental and clairvoyant elements in African palmists and soothsayers and Tarot-tellers!

Feria: Nîmes

> *Feria; cloaked trigonometry of hooves*
> *The plane trees know, shiver with apprehension;*
> *They plead as the archons of the blue steel must*
> *These prayers, refining murder by a breath,*
> *Turn self-deception to an absolution —*
> *Two coloured pawns uniting in the rites of death.*
>
> *Brocade still stiff with bloody hair he kneels*
> *While the mithraic sun sinks in a surf*
> *Of bloody bubbles; leaks from the huge pizzle*
> *The holy urine smoking in the dust.*
> *He reels into a darkness which he dazzles.*
>
> *Tall doors fall as the axes must,*
> *And the great sideboard of the bull is there,*
> *A landslide in the ordinary heart*
> *A feast for gods within a coat of hair,*

Provence

His thunder like a belfry and his roars
The minotaur of man's perfected lust,
His birth-pangs offered to the steel's applause.

When you first come to live here, the ever-present bull-worship of the land seems a somewhat aberrant predisposition, but it does not take very long before this archetypal form stakes a claim on your sympathy by its beauty and its vivid partnership in the activities of man. It has cast the spell of its taurine mystique over human life in unmistakable fashion, whether one is speaking of the giant Iberian bulls which come to be killed in the Spanish-style ritual or of the spry little Camargue animals so famous for their gallantry and cunning, who are not killed but only despoiled of their cockades and strings by the youthful white-clad gladiators called *razeteurs*, whose only weapon is a sort of metal comb, a *razet*. These tiny animals are full of personality. You see them in winter drifting about the fields with a disconsolate, out-of-work look; but the minute the good weather returns and the season promises to open, they become more animated and willing to exchange a few harsh words with any youth brave enough to bull-bait them. In any way at all: sometimes a mischievous dog takes it into his head to mock up a pretend attack and the bull joyfully joins in the game. Or a slightly tipsy villager might propel a wine barrel into the arena with a kick and tease the bull by forcing it to play an impromptu game of football. But when not herded for the bull-game these beautiful creatures drift about like Stone Age messages — as if they had just materialized from the cave drawings of Aurignacian man and reincarnated themselves for the season's sport. Clouds of saffron and brown and charcoal animals people the Languedoc's deserted spaces with an echo of poetry which sends one beyond, into ages of stone, ages of iron. Bull-worship has an almost religious rite, to its credit thought of as a game, yes, but somehow a sacred game with its roots deep in the smiling piety of the French Midi. Our own attraction to it stems from who knows what ancient source within ourselves. The bull was once a sacrificial cult animal. I suspect that after being sacrificed to the requisite god or goddess he was ceremonially cut up, and the whole village fell to with a will and ate him with appropriate libations.

The whole history of the bull and the countries of bull-worship merits a more extended study than these notes, though they will serve me to draw attention to one of the critical pulses of the land. Nobody seems able to decide on the origins of the cult and its close connection with the history of animal sacrifice, though the subject does not lack for fruitful documentation. Yes, the bull is a venerable symbol for the animist and the alchemist, his situation in the zodiac falls between 20 April and 21 May. And one is reminded that in the Middle East one has often seen him harnessed to the plough, and not always castrated. It is a moot point whether the modern bullfight is not a survival which has grafted itself on to some ancient form of blood-worship in which the bull was sacrificed and devoured by a primitive community driven to sheer survival tactics, elaborated into a ritual of worship after its contact with primitive Christianity. But wait! Originally was not the bull coeval with Zeus, and the prime patron of Mithraism? The spread and implantation of this primitive religion is one of the unusual historical factors about old Provence; the Roman army brought it into favour and established it, so much so that it was touch and go whether Mithraism would not prevail over Christianity.

It is odd that despite the history of this double attachment to the bull-game (either the Spanish *corrida* or the so-called *course libre*) we come upon areas of blank, unmapped ignorance about so much of it. The Spanish version of the game is deeply respected and piously played out in gigantic Roman arenas which are ideal on account of size. The distribution of the Spanish style of bullfighting has also varied greatly, at times shrinking to include only the walled mediaeval towns big enough to offer floor-space to the whole elaborate spectacle. The records show that it flowered for a while in unusual sites — Besançon, Macon — and then faded out for a season or two. The Spanish style of bullfight is also encouraged, and its baroque ritualized murder of the great Andalusian bulls is among the more gripping spectacles the Midi has to offer. But few of the bullrings are large enough to allow this elaborate spectacle all the space it needs. The best of the big arenas after Arles is Nîmes, which has always patronized the *mise à mort*; its professionalism has won the approval of the Spanish public as well, and the modern toreador of reputation thinks nothing of crossing the frontier to "play" Nîmes. Nowadays he will gain and not lose face by it. For the *course libre*, which depends upon a free-running bull and a racing man, the Roman arenas are a tiny bit too large and tend to give the bull too much advantage over the racing, white-clad gladiator of the *razet*; for the youth, after making his soaring, plunging snatch at the cockade or slash at the strings tied to the horns, must perforce turn and race for safety from the bull. It is always a narrow shave. His fast flying leap over the barricade and into the very sky — so it seems — is thrilling indeed; for while he hangs like a nest-fallen bird on to the surrounding rails of the arena, the discomfited bull lowers his horns and starts to devastate the arena, sending the planks which line the dusty theatre of the action flying in a glorious clattering cascade. "Aha!" shouts the exultant crowd, "bad temper, eh?" and to salute the animal's mettle the band gives him an extra toot of music through the loudspeakers in the surrounding trees, and the raucous voice of the master of ceremonies announces that the price of the cockade has gone up, thus paying tribute to the extra danger run by the man. Of late years the profession of the *razeteur* has stabilized itself so that you can really make a living in this way. The game has become organized and the quality of the bull-play has correspondingly improved and become more stylish. It is open to anyone who cares to register. (The poet Roy Campbell spent several years in Provence as a *razeteur* and has left us some fine, muscular poetry about the game and a spirited prose book, *Taurine Provence*, which still has flavour and zest, though it is somewhat out of date.)

The humbler world of the *course libre* is close to the heart of Provence — a true test of youthful agility and strength, and a game full of dangers for the unwary. For though the black fighting bulls of the Camargue are small, they wear a large and deadly crown of horns. Moreover, they have seen the man and studied his ways on the range long before they find themselves face to face with him in the ring. And they are cunning as dogs. For the big Spanish bull of the killing fights it is quite another matter, for the first man he sees is the cloak-draped toreador who is sent in to dispatch him. He has no experience of man in battle. But the little Camargue bull lives free on the range with the guardians, and after every fight is decanted back on to the range. In a very short space of time a valiant small bull, realizing that it is not going to be killed but simply played for its cockade, will become a seasoned and cunning adversary. And as he bears a name of his own he steadily forges a career for himself in the world of sport. Several such bulls have shown such bravery, energy and imagination that after their death they have been immortalized by having their statue set up in the village square — like "Sanglier," who gazes benignly across the fields at Villevieille. The Spanish fight with its cumbersome bulls and solemn liturgical ritual belongs to one sort of mood, while the *course libre* breathes all the poetry and energy of youth, springing as it does directly from the land. Together with the tranquil game of *boules*, whose clicking metal balls people the shady forest walks and the esplanades, the cockade fight is the most characteristic activity to be studied in modern Provence, the happiest of open-air sports, glowing with all the ardour of bull-worship. But by and large the two distinct styles have coexisted without prejudice and there is a faithful audience for both.

Yes, the bull-game as patented in the Camargue is fast and somewhat perilous for the man, but in some curious way it feels good-tempered and sporting — even the bull seems to enter into the spirit of the thing, and while there is sometimes an accident, even perhaps a death, the whole poetry of the *course libre* feels human in village terms. It is a sport, while the Spanish style of play is a ritual, a profound and often blood-chilling experience. Perhaps one might compare it with village cricket which has its own time-tested mystique — though one has to see it being played in foreign parts to appreciate its mythological scale of reference and peculiar beauties — like a ballet of the Raj transplanted to Cairo or Corfu.

Though both forms of bull-play are treated with respect, there have always been, will always be, those who find the Spanish *mise à mort*, with its fearsome sword-play and macabre poetry, too much for them simply in terms of blood shed. Others affect to believe that the bull feels very little if he is correctly played by a fine matador with full respect for the science of the kill. It is impossible to judge. Aldo has a tendency to defend the rich Spanish style of bullfight by saying: "Let he who has never asked for his beefsteak to be brought to the table *bien saignant* throw the first stone!" and of course there is hardly anyone who can accept such a challenge.

What is certainly as grisly as it is revealing is the blood-thirsty note of audience participation one gets in Spain to the Spanish type of killings. This kind of hysteric throbbing, sobbing reaction to bull-play seems to stem from some innate avenging lust of the public's super-ego which makes an imaginative psychic link between the savagery and the poetry of the matter — as if mentally feasting on the moral wounds and pouring blood of the great Iberian bulls. For down they go like sinking suns into the ocean of mortal suspense which precedes the killing stroke. Lurching, subsiding, they allow themselves to be demolished like old cathedrals picked to pieces by earthquakes, sinking into the ground like great black concert-grands sinking into a lake of blood and darkness. They seldom roar, though sometimes they offer a groan or sob of reproach to the precise steel of the tricorned gladiator who circles and swerves in his orbit around them, keeping just out of reach, his cloak fluttering like a winnowing fan. The whole of this provisional cloak-play, and the careful planting of the cruel spikes of the fluttering banderillas in certain chosen muscle-schemes of the bull's shoulders, has for objective not only to tire him but to force him through fatigue to lower his great crowned head. Finally he will begin to let his head sag down and this opens a vital hinge of bone in the powerful vertebrae of the animal whose strength is by now half-quenched. (Aldo puts his two fists together and opens a space between knuckles to illustrate.) Thus the way to the heart is open and if the stroke is pure, as they say, and correctly executed, the steel passes through this hinge directly into the heart of the bull and it falls dead as if shot. This is also the famous "moment of truth," for to execute it the matador has to lean forward in a position which for a few seconds renders him vulnerable to a sudden wild lunge from an exhausted but game bull. He may die by an accident: but for the great chimerical animal there is no appeal. There is something ignominious and sad in the way that his body, and that of any horse he has managed to disembowel during the action, are hooked up and dragged away through the dust by the two picadors who are appointed to this task. In defeat he has diminished into a classical hump, a chunk of deflated meat. They slice off his huge advantages according to rule;

only occasionally do they slice off his great smoking pizzle if he has hurt or killed one of his adversaries. Usually just the ears and the tail.

Enough! I am reminded that if anyone expresses any sentiments which suggest distaste for the Spanish style in bullfighting, Aldo takes on an alarmed air, for this is clearly social heresy and out of place in Provence. He places his finger to his lips to admonish the solecism and then waves an arm in the direction of the fireplace over which hangs the magnificent lithograph by the painter Zoravis (once as famous as Picasso) called *Ultimate Truth*, and which depicts the death of a bull in a Spanish *mise à mort*. It seems to be conceived in concentric whorls of the animal's blood. It is full of a noble yet heartrending joy and when the subject comes up Aldo kisses his hand to it, though whether he is praising the artist's excellence or the subject matter of the work I have yet to find out. As for Zoravis, he was eloquent on the beauty of the game and said that it was all mingled up with the image of sacramental blood, the father image and the destruction of the father. A whole galaxy of Freudian images were called to mind by the bull's death; a whole glossary of symbols concerned with sexual power (the blood rite) and the demolition of the father's authority by the son. There was also, by association, the biblical reference concerned with water being turned into wine.

Long ago the painter spent his summers *chez* Aldo, hence the fine collection of lithographs owned by my friend. Zoravis paid for his keep with them. As for water and wine he was no stranger to the latter and I have seen him sometimes quite incapable with drink at the old "Sabre" in Montparnasse, the only bistro except perhaps "La Coupole" which boasted that it could respond to any request, no matter how recondite. The request of Zoravis during his residence in Paris was for a beaker of bull's blood to quaff and this was duly provided by the management around ten o'clock. Zoravis himself was rather a striking-looking old man, not raffish or bohemian at all: more like a respectable diamond broker from Smyrna, say. Nor was he a noisy customer: on the contrary, he drank with thoughtful silence until the hour approached. Then he raised his finger and the old *maître d'hôtel*, who had already betrayed some anxiety, called out in his hoarse voice, "Eh bien, où est le sang du maître?" He would sally out on to the pavement to scan the horizon, gazing up and down with manifest anxiousness. Then at last it hove in sight, the beaker of the *cher maître*. A leather-coated motor-cyclist drew up in front of the café and from his saddlebags produced a tall litre measure — a thermos flask full of dark warm blood. It was wrapped in a spotless napkin and was conveyed thus to the table of the painter who responded with thanks and a banknote which obviously included a tip for the young cyclist, who for his part uttered profound thanks before replacing his goggles and glasses and melting away. Zoravis drank his beaker of blood thoughtfully, judiciously, under the admiring gaze of the young painters-to-be of Montparnasse. This, they felt, was how true greatness should behave! No wonder he had such a reputation for virility!

But of course the real virility was very much there in the great dossier of lithographs drawn from the life at the Feria of Arles over several years, and duly posted up in the high-ceilinged music room and along the broad carpeted galleries leading to it: all the thrilling orchestration of the routine *paseos* touched in with alchemy, the customary eloquence and spareness of the great painter. There is a whiff of the satanic about the execution, due perhaps to the fact that the two leading horsemen are dressed in the grim minatory black of the secret police of Philip II. These are the so-called *alguaciles*: they open the proceedings with an icy formality. Behind them comes the line of the three matadors followed by their assistants with their cloaks and dirks — the *cuadrillas* of *peones*. Lastly, on mettlesome but carefully padded horses, come the

picadors with their lances — the spiked *banderillas* — together
with those delegated to hitch up and drag off the corpse of
the fallen bull or disembowelled horse. These are grim echoes
for an afternoon of brilliant Mediterranean sunlight, and the
theatrical formality and exactitude make it clear that we are
assisting at a ritual and not a mere game, a mere diversion.
Death is in the air. The only concession to colour in this grave
funereal grouping of professional executioners is in the strips
of coloured cloth hanging from the picador's lance. Formally
they pause and salute and wheel before the presidential box
to make their greeting. The band plays enthusiastically. Sol-
emnly the two leaders advance to receive from the presidential hands the great key of the *cagones* where the bulls are
penned; they are waiting to be called into battle. The crowd
cheers with an ever-sharpening impatience, but routine is
routine and must be fully respected, so the performers take
up their positions in line ahead and make a preliminary circuit
to solicit the sympathy and approval of the crowd. At last the
word goes forth and with a dry clang the pen flies open, and
the nearest bull to see the daylight outside plunges from the
darkness like a rocket and swerves into the ring: only to brake
sharply, half-blinded from the daylight, and take up a somewhat hesitant position centre stage, but stamping and ca-
reening with anticipation for he knows not what. Softly,
coaxingly the matadors station themselves and tenderly begin
to position their prey. But lazily, as if they had all the time
in the world. It is puzzling to the bull, their soft tenderness
and amity. He stamps. He smokes!

He cavorts a little, but somewhat shyly, as if he were not
really sure of himself. He is being keenly assessed, judged
for possible weight and stamina: also for any particularities
of deportment. Does he throw to left or right when he
charges? He does not find the general atmosphere reassuring,
but for the moment there seems no real menace, so he does
a preliminary whirl around the ring, putting up a whirligig

of reddish dust, acrid and sour. While he is thus preoccupied the silent circle of matadors slowly gathers together, closes the ring on him without losing the animal tenderness, the feeling of coaxing, and inciting him into the correct position for a first assault on his shoulders. The deltoids are the initial target, his fatigue the first objective. At last it comes: the picadors gallop deftly into the centre and, leaning from the saddle, plant their weapons securely in his massive back. He rears back with the psychological shock of realization and the physical pain of the onslaught. Battle is joined. The whole matter takes on a weight and gravity unforeseen as the blood begins to roll down that target of a back and into the dust. He swells with rage, his pride is wounded — and this is of course what they want. The whole mechanism of the kill begins to unwind itself . . .

Why wait?

Primaeval Camargue horses under sail,
Stealthy as wishes or as secret agents
Curve under Roman monuments, vibrate,
Appropriate to sky as water, sympathetic
As ruins which insist in their serenity
All time could be compressed
Into one pellet of ample duration because
The first step towards creation is to lose
Complete confidence in oneself and sort of die.
I know . . . I see you smile. Accelerate loving.
Remit the old codger's deathbed flutter. Try!
Somehow copy the sweet conduct of these
Young olives in the spring mistral a-quiver
Silverside up with such panache and
Colloquial astonishment in sunset poses.
Join the great coven of real lovers, the

Provence

Conspiracy of lovemates forged in debonnaire
Realized couples like perfected machines
Guided by love-placebos from the wise
        Only realize! Go on! Be wise!
        Yes but how?
They are caressed by oncoming night
With all their nightingales in lovely voice.
And this superb Roman lady asleep
Has the whole pedigree of pure happiness
Delicate as young olives, their pigments,
Loose-leaf in slumber in her smiles.
One becomes sorry to become so soon
Just luggage left like lumber,
Just after-thoughts of inexcusable grace
Posted up by a love-god's outlandish looks,
A love-seraphic smiling face.
Did not the proverb say explicitly
"Never try to whitewash a silk elephant"?
And (beyond all where or why):
"In yoga harness a whole reality with one soft sigh."
A vessel in full sail
With a weird mystical rig
Will tell you once and for all
What the Greek proverb says is true:
"Happiness is just a little scented pig."
It's not enough but it will have to do.

– V –

Caesar's Vast Ghost

Provence remained free and unregimented for much of its life and consequently became a ready seat of dissent; indeed, whatever became too hot to hold in Rome was encouraged to slip over the border and burn itself out in Caesar's favourite bailiwick. Yet when things got out of hand a Roman legion was wont to appear on the scene to restore law and order, as it was known then. Yet the country has remained a crucible of dissent and a prey to conquest from all sides, often in a chronic state of destabilization.

One of the key dates in the history of this part of the world is offered us by the founding of Marseille in 600 BC. This was perhaps the most important trading post thrown down by the Greeks in their drive westward, beyond the pillars of Hercules. The town which grew upon this horn of promontory was stamped with their particular genius. Of the founding there is a delightful legend which recounts how the Phocean leader Protis, in order to negotiate the founding of a city, sought the good offices of Nannus, King of the Segobriges. This latter was at that moment busy marrying off a daughter, and custom dictated that at the wedding banquet she must present a drink to the suitor of her choice as a mark of her acceptance. She opted for the handsome stranger and her decision was respected. So was the town born, the colony founded.

The obvious function of the first colony was to straddle the transoceanic route for tin, which was then firmly in Phoenician control, using the waterways offered by the Rhône. They were implicitly aiming their influence in the direction of the oppidum of Mont-Lassois, the main tin market situated between Saône and Seine. Gradually Marseille established sub-colonies on the coast and one or two toeholds inland to guard communications there. She even set up shop for her wares in the suburbs of Arles (at Trinquetaille).

But this flourishing traffic seems to have gradually come to a standstill from the beginning of the fifth century, probably due to the internal upheavals of the Celtic tribes. Marseille seemed to have suffered an eclipse despite the brilliant explorations of Euthymenos Africa-wards on the gold and ivory trails, not to mention the equally brilliant forays of Pytheas northwards on the routes traced by the amber and the tin. Yet it would be fair to regard Marseille as the sentinel of Rome in Gaul, and when in real trouble (as with the Ligurians) she always persuaded Rome to intervene in her favour and save the day. This convenient alliance only came to an end with the siege of Caesar. He had set up his headquarters in Arles, which was then (so hard to imagine today) a flourishing seaport with shipyards which he used to start building a fleet. It was a convenient springboard from which to invest the ill-prepared city which, despite its collapse, remained always a lively capital, living on its wits and its past reputation for intellectual brilliance. Commercially, however, Narbonne gradually rose in eminence, and then Arles.

But despite its decline, the old Greek colony kept its paradoxical reputation for alertness and originality: it was something between a watering-place, a spa, and a place of choice for political exiles or dissenters who had got into trouble with the authorities. One's thoughts turn to the remarkable tribute to the city recorded in the pages of Livy (Book XXXVII: 54):

"If national character could be subdued and modified by what I will call the genius of place, the people of Massilia would long since have reverted to savagery from contact with so many uncultured nations which surround them. But on the contrary they enjoy as much respect and consideration as if they lived in the plumb centre of Greece. In truth it is not only because of the purity of the language they speak, or of their style in dress, but above all their customs, their legislation and their national character which they have kept intact and pure, free of all foreign contamination."

Indeed, that intangible factor, a national predisposition, hangs on despite all change, in the most obstinate manner: I was intrigued to find that the Greek–Roman polarity was equally discernible in modern terms in the Dodecanese Islands (where I served on the Administration for a couple of years). These Greek islands had been in Italian possession for almost half a century, and had been turned into a Roman playground for summer holidaymakers. Yet Greek frugality and spareness contrasted with the uxorious and imaginative Roman way of life exactly as in ancient times. The Greeks moved from improvisation, brilliantly inventive, but tight-rope-walking. The Romans evolved an unhurried discipline, a dignity and order which obviated all panic.

Jérôme was particularly acute when it came to judgements bearing upon the contrasts between the Roman and Greek character, for of course both were Mediterranean and so complementary rather than antithetical. They needed each other's support, for their conduct and attitude gave diversified results, and the differences between them were striking. Temperamentally, Greece was a sea-animal, and Rome a land-animal.

Provence

It all, as Jérôme liked to say, came down to landscape as a determinant of character: the Greeks were born in a barren land, and with a character inured to physical privation. Greek and Roman experience were situated on different axes of experience. The Roman was the land-animal, yes, but he sprang from a landscape which was rich and full of variety. His was not bare Greek island stone, half blind with the violet frenzy of Aegean light; it was a rolling verdant land rich with every imaginable kind of tillage: rich in forests and harvests, in rivers and hills. The Greek mind was fuelled by an overwhelming curiosity, avid for truth rather than for gain, and superstitious to the core; moreover, the Greek mind was entrenched behind the complicated syntax of a language that was both allusive and abstract, both complicated to learn and rich to exploit scientifically in ideas. The Greeks were headlong about things, whether in exploration or adventure. They did not fear the injudicious, for they allowed themselves to be carried away by curiosity. And they were brave to the point of foolhardiness: navigators and explorers indulging a thirst for novelty. They planted some trees, to be sure, fruit trees of every sort and — like a note in music — the first olive trees! They went ahead with plans for deforestation and cultivation, but essentially they were not people of the interior. They did not colonize, tranquillize, civilize the lands they visited, but travelled along, content to secure the sea-roads, reconnoitre the ports and estuaries, and to establish trading posts firmly set upon naval lines of communication: Arles, Nice, Antibes, Agde . . . a tenuous chain of point events. The sea-animal was hunting for other things, its mariners were restless. Their curiosity was to push them through the Strait of Gilbraltar, and if legends are to be believed, carry them round the British Isles. But their feeling for Provence, though ardent, was of shallow provenance; they were traders, yes, but they traded like mariners.

Despite their shallow penetration — for they always seem

to have settled along the sea-coast — they were sufficiently influenced by the Roman taste for consolidation to declare Massilia a republic. It was to become famous for the wisdom of its laws and a model which influenced many subsequent republics. Perhaps the founders were, after all, local dignitaries rejoicing in a touch of Roman *gravitas*. At any rate the two psychologies, the two mental dispositions, made common cause in many things. The variegated composite which resulted in the Provençal character was enriched by such variety. But as with most of the Greek enterprises, the taming and consolidating of the hinterland waited upon the Roman armies which would one day secure and develop these inland communications which connected Marseille with Geneva.

In contrast to the Greeks, the Roman believed in history, in permanence, and this assurance became part of his affective life, his confidence in land and water, in husbandry and in time. The Roman's character was a lazy one, his language a grave lapidary one, his temperament less that of poet than of grammarian, jurist, law-giver, moralist. His bent was for stock-taking, ancestor-worship. The Romans were jurists and land-surveyors at heart, worshippers of the cadastral survey, children of the milestone! The infantry of the line was nourished by the deeply felt and embedded uxoriousness of the Roman ideal whose form of art was expressed in the poetry of function (Pont du Gard). It is not possible even today to look upon those great mortarless arches in petrolithic honey without emotion. They are hymns to the Goddess of Water!

The numerous festivals and recitals of all kinds provide frequent surprises. For example, I recall being urged to attend a performance of *Holiday on Ice* in the Nîmes arena. I discovered that they had flooded the arena in true Roman fashion and frozen it into a skating rink. The performance, beautifully lit and orchestrated, was literally breath-taking; and to see this on a moonlit night in August, in such a setting, was downright moving! I had forgotten that the original construction had allowed for sea-battles: the whole arena was turned into a lake on such occasions. I had only remembered the disagreeable orgies of bloodlust which provided the standard variety of entertainment for the general public in the ages of Roman primacy. There are some tremendous massacres on the records and it is not possible to read about them without feeling that the Romans had a streak of vicious callousness in their make-up. Gladiatorial combat is one thing, but feeding helpless captives or slaves to wild animals in order to relish their distress, that is something else. It is more than likely that the Greeks felt a twinge of distress, of disgust, at the weight of Roman philistinism, and the crudeness with which these brutal spectacles were played out before an audience of ordinary citizens. It threw into relief the markedly different life-styles of the Romans and the Greeks, illustrated from the outset by the sharply differing syntax of Latin and Greek. The Roman temper was at the base juridical and moralistic, strong on jurisprudence and the codification of civic morals. The Greek was less exact but more profound. The contrast must have been even more accentuated in ancient times: I suppose that the Greek lateen-rig whaler contrasted markedly with the lumbering Roman galley with its forest of slave-propelled oars, though perhaps the latter could count on eight to nine knots of speed. But the lighter Greek craft could be drawn up on the beach if need be.

The same contrast in style and preoccupation could doubtless have been discerned in the two different orientations of theatre. The Greek production was anxious about human identity face-to-face with God or with the bias of nature; a whole community struggling to realize itself in terms of mystical identity could purge itself of its fears at one and the same time. The absolution was in the catharsis. The Roman was preoccupied with the theme of appropriate conduct and human destiny. It was anchored firmly in time and in the circumstantial. It breathed all the idealism of a perfected civic code. It investigated right and wrong with fidelity and poetic felicity. The Roman range of concern is less profound, more bourgeois in the modern sense, and expresses itself best in moral concern for the human situation. The gods and goddesses exist, but as beautiful and evocative illustrations of a nature which was a friend and a lover, not a rather terrifying repository of metaphysical terrors and philosophical truths. The two poetries point up these differences in stark fashion. The theatre productions and their plays emphasize the radical difference of bent: Greek catharsis and Roman absolution through virtuous conduct and civic uprightness. The contrast reflects itself in the very structure of their theatres, for the Greek is breathlessly abstract, sophisticated in its spiritual insight and its endless questing for metaphysical truth, while the Roman seems content to aspire to an understanding of civic virtue and moral worth through the human situation. It needs very little imagination to gaze through the Roman theatre of Orange, for example, and see (as if at the end of a telescope) the Greek theatre of Epidauros with its supreme equipoise. But they were two different codes, two different ways of looking at human history and the contemporary reality. Provence has enjoyed both styles of mind, both types of sensibility.

Thus the Roman experience feeds back into the Greek and vice versa, and the sensitive observer can take the measure of both and glory in them separately, for each culture brought with it the fruit of original insight, and a creative distress which still echoes on in these stone remains. In 1837, Stendhal, in a brief jotting, recorded his admiration for the blithe purity of the Maison Carrée of Nîmes in the following words: "The overall effect is admirable. I have seen more imposing monuments in Italy itself, but nothing as pretty as this *pretty antique*, even though rather overcharged with ornamental detail, which however doesn't exclude the beautiful. It's the smile of someone who is habitually serious." He had sensed something like the particular magic of an archetypal form expressing itself through a mere copy: the convention of a Roman studio. It was an aching reminiscence of a forgotten style of stone rapture which the formal and functional Roman life-style had overlaid and set aside.

(Yet how obstinate the archetypal pattern is: it repeated itself in the gladiatorial stance of the wrestler or boxer, the equipoise of the dancer, the crafty and dissolute face of the Camargue gypsy, or the moronic and lustreless gaze of the toreador raised to virtual heroism as he strikes home. Not to mention such constants of place as the beauty of the Arles girls: each looks as if she had been freshly wished and love-minted to order. The little Christmas *santons** of Provence with their butcher-baker-candlestick-maker preoccupations must echo the same concern with the persistence of archetypes through the different vocations.)

* * *

Pictograms:
Julius Caesar, Augustus, Agrippa, Marius, Olive, Hannibal, Dante, Tiberius, Marquis de Sade, Petrarch, Charles Martel, Laura, Mistral, Marius the general, Justine, Mireille . . .

In the margins some notes by Aldo, which I suppose were due to be added in due course. Tibullus was of equestrian rank and inherited an estate unlike most of the poets: but he lost most of it when Mark Antony and Octavian confiscated land for the soldiers' bounties. Virgil, Propertius and Horace all suffered in this way, while Ovid's gaffe was the most

---

*From Provençal *santoun*, "little saint," the name for figurines in coloured plaster used to decorate the Christmas crib. There are far more of these than in the traditional crib as we know it. They portray all sorts of Provençal village characters.

expensive one of all and resulted in an exile which ruined his life. How sad that we will never know what it was. Alas!

Somebody commented on the number of generals who figure in his check-list, whereupon Aldo defended himself by saying: "When Caesar was reproached for his well-known keenness for battle he said: 'Only in battle does one realize that no one can do your dying for you: as in love you realize that nobody can do your loving.' " Very apt. But I have been unable to find the reference anywhere — Livy, Tacitus and so on, I have combed them in order to track it down. Is it possible he made it up?

In 121 BC the vassal province called Gallia Narbonensis was founded. To achieve this provisional peace Caesar had been forced to conquer 800 towns, force 300 tribes to plead submission, to kill more than a million souls of the civil populations, enslave another million while declaring the rest (about the same number) to be "Roman citizens." If anyone was competent to pronounce upon the effects of war it was surely Caesar.

Actually Aldo's account of Caesar is not entirely implausible; nations realize themselves after traversing a crisis of national identity in which their existence is put to risk. A battle won provides the oxygen necessary to vindicate their continued existence, the triumphant self-realization which constitutes the almost religious sense of identity which thereafter cannot be controverted. One thinks of the Armada or the Battle of Britain in 1940 — what they did for the English image and national self-respect. Similarly, in cobbling up the history of this land one can see how the great battles of history contributed fruitfully to push forward the crisis of national identity which nourished each and every historic manifestation. Greek identity was finally ratified by the definitive destruction of the Persian army (Salamis), as Roman identity was due to the victory over Greece. Not to mention the stunning effect of a battle like Actium with its sudden, indeed inexplicable, rout of the Egyptian fleet. Nor must we forget that Caesar's fleet had been built to specification in the famous shipyards of Arles, a town which then straddled an estuary and had easy access to the sea! Moreover, after the defeat of Cleopatra at Actium the same fleet was recalled and ordered to lie up at its winter anchorage under the walls of Fréjus. How odd these dispositions seem to us today! The profile of the land and the coastline have altered so much that we can only recall them by a deliberate act of the imagination. Yet despite all these fantasies and projections one catches a glimpse of what Provence must have meant to the ancients — a sort of Tibet-shaped land of paradisiacal luxuriance, remote and at peace.

Aldo is apt to say, "You may be sure that of the two styles of bullfight, Caesar would have favoured the grimmer and the more colourful — the Spanish!"

"He nowhere says so, Aldo!"

"Hush, my dear boy! When reality tends to become more and more ignominious, surely one has the right to give it a tiny French polish? Caesar is one of the cult heroes of this country. He was a queer customer and ushered in a new order of sensibility. He was the complete bisexual without shame or false vainglory, 'husband of all women and wife to all men,' as the chroniclers record it. Seen from our own vantage-point in time it would seem to us that he owed his magnificent control to an overwhelming psychic frigidity. This lent a strange peculiarity to the affair with Cleopatra. The fact that both parties were homosexual led to a strange inversion; he played with her the role of the woman who has intercourse with a man. This bound them together very closely. It was their secret. We know this type of love which has been decoded and described by other inquirers. Those movements only interest him at coitus which resemble the twitching of the death-throes. In contrast to his fantasies of violence experienced in dreams is the fact that his potency disappears if his partner moves. She must stay still, grow pale, tremble, and as far as possible resemble a corpse . . . It is perhaps from a sharp awareness of this predisposition that the order was given to compose the Imperial perfume in his honour — the celebrated Telinum, at once bitter and mildly sweet, which was very much to his taste. Its base was of honey, marjoram, rose-hips, fenugreek and balm, and the preparation was mingled with wine which made it tenacious of application. Alcohol was not as yet used with the range available to the upper-class Roman society woman. But the records speak of the hours she spent at the hairdresser having her curls shaped by the hot iron.

"The Roman society woman operated according to an elaborate code of ornament in which perfume played an exact and exacting role. She went to parties with her forehead and forearms painted white, lips and cheeks coloured ochre, eyelids and the surrounding of the eye itself touched in with the black powder of antimony. She was not afraid to mix scents and she had a great anthology of perfumes from which to select her weapons. The names alone reveal a good deal: the Cyprinum from Cyprus, the Metopium, the Myrthum-Laurum, the Susinum, the celebrated Rhobinum which was obtained by the elaborate maceration of the roses of Rhodes in various unguents, not to mention the most famous, which was called Scent of Kings and composed of some thirty rare unguents! But the one that Caesar never wearied of was the slightly acid-spicy Telinum: when Cleopatra wanted to please him, or before asking for a favour, she held out her hands to be sprinkled with this Imperial composition. Her acceptance of this scent was equivalent to according him an intimate caress — though of course every exchange between them partook of calculation. There was no love lost between them, but boundless admiration ruled them. When during their intimacies he began to address her as 'my sister,' she found the sexual stimulus she sought.

"As for herself, it was some time before she revealed the secret of her power as a ruler. It was bound up with magic. She had an extra small toe on her left foot, a withered little appendix, but something by which one could swear or cast spells. She had often had a mind to get the excrescence amputated by the barber surgeon who attended her, but so great was his superstition that she could not persuade him to execute her command — even though the price of refusal could be death for disobedience. Seeing his terror and perplexity she told him as much, ordering him to caress the object and let her formulate a wish on it as he did so. What the wish was no one would ever know — so she said. But the upshot of the whole matter was that her surgeon found himself paying the price of his cowardice — thrown to the lions in the arenas together with a rabble of slaves and Christians!

"Just to complicate matters, woman is born awake and man asleep. After she has woken him with her kiss he puts her to sleep in another dimension, the fifth, which opens on to futurity. History starts to get born when the couple's love is in phase, their orgasms simultaneous and wired to the senses by synchromesh. Woman loves the personality of the man, in him she 'reads' the infant she will create and awaken. He loves the nature of woman, she he elects as a mother. She decodes his flesh and he her heart. The bazaars of the affect unite. The orgasm is the heart's pacemaker, peacemaker, the blood's timepiece. Our knowledge of chronicity derives from the womb-imprinted rhythms.

"The two ugly bitches Combustion and Traction rule our world. (Crossing himself he muttered, 'Heat over mass equals light. Amen!') And so saying he climbed on her, praying that the sutra would work." Later on during that summer Aldo received the fatal *déclic* and at last felt himself becoming incapable of any more grief! He had started residing as appropriately as the fruit of a poem in this new griefless state. For so long Aldo had thought that getting old and dying were things that happened to others. The shock of realization was so great that he burst out laughing, and then grew rueful.

*   *   *

It is impressive to catch little glimpses of the newly hatched European sensibility slowly evolving from all these contradictory persons and impulses. Someone who could stand the organized butchery of the Roman arenas, in all its rabid coarseness, would clearly not have any reservations regarding a Spanish-style bullfight today, though psychologically the "bread and circuses" formula was a means of crowd control, a way of sating the popular bloodlust of the Roman mob — Caesar's military instruments.

They discovered that in each of us there lives another who is the precise counterpart of ourselves; in the other sex we love this counterpart. Thus, for love of our own sex we try to run away from that very counterpart. The duality of the instinct is not split in the human soul: mother instinct, for example, and hatred of motherhood coexist in the human heart. The homosexual woman always shows involuntarily her hatred of motherhood because she cannot help it. So the man. All this was to be rediscovered through a systematic reappraisal of human behaviour and motives in their social and political contexts. Politics is simply the blueprint which encourages all these secret predispositions to evolve into action. And of course a whole civilization, especially one which elaborated itself so carefully in social and sexual formulae, does not fall apart overnight — it disintegrates slowly, reluctantly, purposefully. And nowhere does one manage to trace its various strains and stresses so clearly as in prevailing sexual habits and beliefs, judged by the conventional Freudian hindsight of our time. The future may modify it one day, but for the moment it is as far as we can see and we dare not ignore it. The so-called homosexual neurosis is a flight back to one's own sex! The basic throbbing motive turns out to be based in a powerful protective wall against the promptings of man's own criminal self. In truth, his attitude towards woman is characterized by a tremendous hatred which he dare not admit. In dreams he figures as the wild bear who attacks women, strangles them, drinks their blood! The bear is his own image, and a symbolic warning . . . for blood is his true need, his deepest requirement. Spermatic fluid, urine, faeces . . . they are all dream-substitutions which represent blood! Caesar's ghosts!

As Stekel notes: "We have seen with what powerful hatred the homosexual encounters his environment. Whether he turns his hatred towards the other sex, his own, or under certain circumstances against himself, he remains the inveterate hater trying to reconcile the feelings of man's aboriginal nature with the ethical requirements of later culture. The question arises, whether he is at all capable of really loving. No, the truth is that he is unable to love! That peculiarity he shares with all artists who are in fact also incapable of loving. Poets formulate a longing for love precisely because of their inability to love, and that drives them to a continuous chase after love-adventures. True love becomes the poet's unattainable ideal. The poet differs from the criminal only because he is aware of his incapacity to love as a handicap, and from hatred and scorn of humanity turns to love his fellows."

But the great definitive point of sheer cleavage in the evolution of the European psyche seems to have come with monotheism and the decline of the old comfortable Roman world of nymphs and gods. Yes, with the gradual faltering end of the Roman inspiration, they came: the auctioneers, the Semitic doctors of divinity, sliding about in the undergrowth of the Word like serpents — busily setting up a new and repellent doctrine based on guilt and repentance, sin and self-punishment, self-mutilation. This reforming programme began its work of moulding the new psyche, which in turn would undertake the social and political changes in the body politic of the Europe-to-be. Guilt, original sin, circumcision, atonement. And all symbolized by the blood-spattered crucifix with its nailed-up symbol of man's divinity, the holy predicament of twentieth-century man! Surely it is unique among religions known to history: they have always tended to anchor themselves in natural forms and forces — sun, moon, stars, etc. They opted for a relationship with nature. But this veering away towards a thirst for pre-eminence offers us the first faint silhouette of an approaching scientific materialism — impossible to avoid the feeling of a premonitory depression as one realizes that the final battle for the consciousness of European man (no less) has been joined, and that behind the scenes what is happening is that the Torah is trying to swallow and digest the Hindu scriptures, the Upanishads! The struggle is absolute and the fear is that while the Semitic power may well lose and be overwhelmed, it will succeed in dragging European thought down into ruin by its force — the Luciferian principle of Judaism contains this gloomy power. And of course the chief question to be faced is always the same one: are you interested in trying to secure happiness, well-being for yourself and those around you, or would you rather revel in distress? One day you ask your dark angel in a whisper: "Is happiness after all built-in? Is death finally redeemable?" And the whole pattern of your life is determined by whether it answers yes or no! Caesar must have said to himself one day: "Woman is nature's most amazing gamble." But he simply could not predict the turn of events, the evolution of the historical principle. (Often she wore no paint whatsoever on her brow . . . just left those fine mammalian eyes to speak for her, like a bird of prey, both proud and crafty.)

Les Saintes

It has rained all night on the lake
Until the swans burst out in uncontrollable
Sobs of pleasure and the vertical
Summer moon arrived on cue —
So much explicit wonder soft as silk:
Consenting adults expressing lively doubts,
Lovers with time, and not enough to do!

Here I am, lost in wonder at the self-evident.
Anointed by vexations — alone!
The hardest thing is to get used to the thought
"It had to happen this way and no other!"
Why not then this beautiful available whore?
You could die in such arms with no loss
Of carnal self-respect. Ask for Cunégonde!
She comes with a rope and nothing more,
Thirsty for pre-eminence like all her tribe,
The carotid caressed prepared her for the stake,
Genetics of a human doubt or loss of hope
Is something we could do without or slake
Defunct punks buried with disjunct monks
A PhD in sorrow paid in full by time.
The town clocks mark the hours chime by chime
As chunk by chunk they bury liquid time.

The various temperamental differences evolved gradually against a landscape of contrasts and images; the Swiss glaciers swelling the forest-lined rivers in their drive to the sea, propelling the water through successive layers of earth, mineral to begin with, so that the whole Crau is packed with rock specimens like the cabinet of a mineral expert (the Museum of Minerals at Alès is unique in Europe): hence the rich soils in all their lowland fertility. The limestone glades of central

Provence with their welcoming atmosphere, which seduced the builder's temperament and made it develop the resources of stone (Agrippa): imperishable monuments in mortarless marble.

But of course the Rhône valley is a tunnel, a great ravine, and its delta blocks its issue like a sponge-bag, forcing it to overflow and divert its riches to right and left of its course. There is food for grim thought in the fact that for some 300 kilometres of this famous valley, 'twixt Malville (Isère) and Marcoule (Gard) one can count no fewer than six major nuclear sites of civil or military consequence: the heaviest nuclear concentration of such installations in the western world!

Provence, then, was not merely an apposite metaphor of a name, but it was also a recipient in which these various social and human strains (like different musical instruments) found a troubled harmony and lineage. Moreover, it has always remained a separate place with an identity of its own despite all the echoes which go to furnishing its particular psychology and ethos. Mistral invented nothing — he described what was there, spread before his vision. Neither did Rabelais with the sacred Abbey of his Provençal vision. The Roman, with his thirst for permanence and his respect for history, matched the Greek's impatience with limits, his thirst for novelty, his preference for poetry over divination.

When I reproach Aldo for his extravagant Caesar-worship he becomes plaintive and insists that "to get anywhere near human truth you must always over-simplify," and it's possible that there is something authentic in his portrait of the pale preoccupied chieftain limping back and forth across this river-beset land rehearsing in his mind all the many problems not of statecraft but of pure logistics: food and fodder for foreign cavalry, forests decimated for the shipyards of Arles, quarries excavated for the building programmes of Nîmes, Orange, Avignon . . .

And of course under the superficial shadow-play of events

the history of the landscape was busy trying to realize itself, to express its innermost predisposition through the various actors who occupied the stage. We had begun to accept the existence of the various temperaments — Roman, Greek, Persian, African, Spanish, Frank, Gaulish, German, British. Yet underneath it all remained the persuasive intuition of Provence as a sort of laboratory in which the European sensibility was perpetually trying to forge itself anew: with each new race or strain the fitful light of the land played upon the newcomer, refashioning his attributes of soul, remodelling his capacities in the field of civic virtue as well as his competence in matters of love and insight!

In the hinterland the great historic hinge was opening upon new landscapes. The Roman world was falling into its long-announced decline. The real flashpoint of the new civilization was a basic principle, an article of philosophic belief which one can sum up as monotheism — but this after decades of religious skirmishing and bitter debate over alternative paths of conduct. At one period it even seemed that religions like Mithraism might carry the day and establish themselves in place of the nascent Christian faith. But it is most probable that the superior energy and determination shown by the proponents of Judaism were responsible for masterminding the new age. Monotheism carried folded within it the shade of monosexualism, and the new philosophies were slanted upon a new vector in which the homosexual psyche found a new theatre of operations for itself in spheres like politics and statecraft. The struggle that followed was a determined one — an energetic Judaism came out against homosexuality, invoking the social motive loud and clear.

– VI –

Nurse and Mistress of the Crossroads

The only vexation for the visitor to Provence is to discover with dismay that he has not enough time to do justice to all the country has to offer in the way of historic monuments; they are as numerous as they are various, but it is not possible to see everything in Avignon or Nîmes or Arles in a brief visit. Each would require a minimum week or ten days to achieve a thorough feeling of familiarity. The ideal would be actual residence for a few weeks out of season, but how many of us can hope for such a thing?

The best and most methodical way of dealing with the pleasures these towns have to offer is to tackle them in constellations of three or four, for they tend to group themselves as such and the distances between them are not great. You can lie at Avignon, for example, and have a day's shopping in Arles or Nîmes with no pressure on your driving times, and with plenty of time to spare for lunch *en route*. But from all these grand towns you will certainly be tempted to elect Arles as the most exciting in its various beauties, perched as it is on the edge of a watery delta with its back to the infernal mistral. Both the present pre-eminence of Arles as a historic and folkloric centre, and its store of lovely Roman monuments, make it seem far and away the most centralized spot from which to commence an investigation of the Midi's charms, whether Roman, Christian, or Mistralian. There are, of course, several keys to the Roman experience — cities which flourished under imperial rule — but perhaps the most important for us today is dusty, sunburnt Arles at the end of its cobweb of motorways. It is the Queen Mother of the group and has a great diversity of monuments and singularities to offer the visitor. It is usually regarded as the most picturesque city in the whole of Provence and this may be correct. It is in Arles that one should experience one's first cockade-snatching bullfight, a wild village game turned into a great sport and depicted on the Greek vases of Crete in full verisimilitude.

The virtue of such a beginning will become obvious when one wants to extend one's travels, for Arles is like a starfish in a central position, extending its arms in all directions. It is unbeatable as a central axis for local explorations, and very specially the vestiges of ancient Rome. Indeed the standard cadastral reconstruction of the Roman town which is based on old Arles is an admirable tool of reference for the whole group of towns, for they all enjoy analogous features and dispositions and help one walk about "inside the picture," and to feel oneself a temporary Roman going about one's lawful occasions in a Roman setting. It is faithful to such different localities as Nîmes, Aix, Orange, Vaison la Romaine, St-Rémy, as well as to Carpentras and Cavaillon. More recent studies still have discovered a powerful ally in the aerial photography of ancient sites; one can read the traces of foundations and lines of communications on a Roman site for they print up on a photographic plate like teeth in the camera of a dental surgeon.

In historic time, Arles, which lies near the apex of a triangle formed by the sheltering branches of the Rhône, was bathed on one side by the river by which she received merchandise from the north, and on the other side by the lagoons (the

Celtic word is *lôn*, or *lyn*) with their submerged land which extended to the sea. When the famous general Marius (of whom we have more to relate) had connected up these lagoons with his strategic canal, Arles found that it could import and export merchandise destined for the whole Mediterranean. In Roman times the Camargue was a second Egypt, for the whole of its 20,000 acres was regularly inundated by the Rhône. It was called the granary of the Roman army, while flourishing little Arles was designated "The Breasts," so abounding in plenty was she supposed to be. It is worth noting that the coastal Greek and Roman cities are not sited on the actual coast itself, on the river bars, but on the lagoons which were deep then and afforded safe anchorage for merchant ships. These lagoons, through which both fresh and salt water flowed, were always healthy in classical times; but wind and wave and alluvium tended to block their seaward mouths and convert them into stagnating marshland exhaling malaria. During the Middle Ages no attention was paid to this fact, and stations which had been perfectly wholesome in the classical epoch were rendered pestilential, and the cities dwindled in size to clusters of fever-smitten hovels. The situation deteriorated steadily and it was Louis XIV who finally called for an engineering survey of the region which resulted in the decision to strengthen the Rhône embankments. Recently surveys suggest that this was not the answer to the problem, and the whole matter is under discussion at government level.

As for the ordinary citizenry of Arles, it prides itself on the purity of its original and unbroken descent, as witness the reputation of its female beauty. But long before the Romans there was unquestionably a Gaulish settlement on the site, as witness the early Celtic name *Ar-larh* or "moist habitation." This was seemingly occupied by the Greeks — and in the original race Greek and Gaulish strains combined. Then in 46 BC a Roman colony was planted on the site. Caesar decided that he must pay off his debts of gratitude to the officers and men of his armies in the time-honoured fashion, with gifts of land. He ordered Claudius Tiberius Nero, one of his questors, father and grandfather of the Emperors Tiberius Claudius and Caligula, to lead two expeditions into Provence and take up a colonial station at Narbonne and at Arles. This was therefore one of the first military colonies to be planted outside the frontiers of Italy.

The mission of this Tiberius was to portion out the land equitably among Caesar's veterans of the Sixth Legion, some 6,000 officers and men. The ensuing settlement was christened Arelate Sexantorum. We are lucky to have from the pen of Tacitus a description of the procedure to be followed on such occasions. After the tribunes and the centurions came a cloud of minor officials called *agrimensores* or surveyors who undertook the technical side of things, the actual parcelling-out of the sites among the newcomers. Hard on their heels followed a hierarchy of civil officers, religious, judicial or administrative, all under the direction of an administrator-general who bore the title *curator coloniae*. From that moment onwards the transformation of the little colony into a little Rome was only a matter of time!

In next to no time the new arrivals set about building a capitol, a forum, temples, triumphal arches, aqueducts, markets — and in the longer term, theatres, a circus, public baths. In a very few years the outward aspect of Arles was brought into line with the Roman life-style of its founders. A mercantile city of Graeco-Gauls had become Latinized, bureaucratic, and flattered itself that it was cast in the image of the new parent on the Tiber. It even got itself rechristened as Gallula Roma, Arelas (the Roman Gaul). What we see today is a far cry from the flourishing colonies which left their print upon the manners and character of this mixture of lawless tribes; their slow deterioration, their spoliation is heart-rending to contemplate.

The commercial power of ancient Arles in the time of Caesar made it a formidable rival to Marseille. Its population is said to have numbered 100,000 souls. But until Caesar decided to demolish and despoil Marseille, Arles remained under the thumb of the rival city, paying customs dues to it for all navigation. He was punishing Marseille for having sided with Pompey in the recent squabble between them. With the defection of Marseille the way was clear for a bit of diplomatic manoeuvring and Caesar, having dispatched his rival, turned all his gratitude upon Arles. (He very conveniently overlooked the fact that powerful naval units from the Arles fleet lent an active hand to Hannibal when he was crossing France — an attack which nearly wiped out Rome.) He directed that Arles should inherit all the wealth and all the political pre-eminence that had belonged to Marseille, and from that moment prosperity set in for the little place. Wealth followed the new privileges conferred by him.

But nothing lasts for ever, and the ravaged shell of Arles which we have today attests only too clearly to the barbarian visitations (Visigoths, Saracens) which have defaced a once beautiful city. The arenas are the largest in Europe but in a wretched state of preservation, compared for example to the lovely ancient theatre of Orange. It is with sinking heart that one reads descriptions of the city at the height of its prosperity. The original bridge of boats which traversed the Rhône has of course disappeared in favour of a modern one. It was extolled for its beauty and importance by Ausonius no less, a poet who afterwards espoused the Garonne as his inspiration for the long and admirable poem which was his lifework. But one can read it with equal appropriateness while keeping in mind the Rhône — the great rivers are not too dissimilar, though the Rhône is by far the more evocative and distinctive as poetic subject matter, or so I think.

Arles is a city grouped round a hamlet, whose charms can be savoured by a short walk in any direction. Its past, like its future, is bound up with the Rhône and the cultures of the Rhône; it was a flourishing seaport with famous shipyards where the fleets of Caesar and Antony and the rest were fashioned from timber floating down the Rhône. The shipyards must have been all that historians say they were, for when Caesar ordered his fleet to be built there (the one with which he defeated Pompey) it was fitted out and delivered in less than a month, an unheard-of speed. Deforestation must have begun even at that early date. It was to turn the Rhône valley slowly into a wind-tunnel down which the mistral screams and shudders today. In 2,000 years, however, the sea has receded some 28 miles, and what was a flourishing seaport is now a dusty and somewhat moribund little town upon a sandy estuary, shouldered by the passing currents of the great river which once used to empty itself into the blue Mediterranean at this point. It must have been a splendid and airy city with its grouped frieze of handsome monuments, all of them in public use and consequently alive against a flourishing background of commerce and artisan labour. Moreover, commercial and military strategy made it the concern of emperors. Clear air, clear skies and cleansing winds kept it free from the scourges of silted-up estuaries and stagnant dikes which encourage today's mosquitoes. The views which presented themselves in every direction were matchless in their beauty. The high rocks and spurs of Montmajour, now high and dry, formed a massive and impregnable island barrier to the south. But there is still movement and light today, specially where the Rhône girdles the town with all its slow dignity.

The hazards of Caesar's war with Pompey made Arles rich, but much was also due to the strategic position the town occupied at the junction between the three principal highways of the Roman world, the Via Domitia, Via Aurelia and Via Agrippa. She thoroughly deserved her nickname as "nurse and mistress of the crossroads." Moreover, Rome once more exercised its water magic and gave the little town something it most conspicuously lacked: an aqueduct of 46 kilometres, traversing valleys and hills to bring fresh water to it from the Alpilles, while the Rhône itself was broached with a siphoning process to purify the residential suburb of Trinquetaille, nowadays shabby enough, in all conscience, but then the chic residential suburb where richer Romans had holiday houses or sent their families to escape the heat of the coast.

Trinquetaille

Encouraged by red wine, at Equiconque,
Fête votive of a Roman village on water
Cartoons of human licence at play
The dancers hairy cherubs, thimbles for lips
Infatuated by this glorious termagant
Her mass of blonde tragedienne's spitcurls
Worn like a ponytail, parted lips and thighs,
Fecundity without blemish, kisses in hot wax,
Her partner a mock-up of urban man
A horizontal giggle bursting its banks.
The important thing you felt was: learn to hesitate.
                    Dancer!
Kept alive on placebos in his prime
The old love-boobies, laureates of lust,
Eros amans, his boy-love is a must,
Deaf in one eye, the sacred Third,
Blind in one ear he dances in the dust
All the secret histories make it clear
Caesar was once happy here.

The old Roman bridge, to judge by its remains, must have been a wonderful feat of aesthetic engineering. Alas! the modern bridge which greets the traveller is an eyesore. One is not consoled even to find oneself in the little suburb of Trinquetaille with its echoes of Rabelais. Yet it must not be forgotten that the Arles crossing was a capital communications link for the Romans. The Via Aurelia, which extended from Rome to Cadiz, took Arelate in its stride. The modern autoroutes in some places are sited upon the foundation of the old Roman roads, and the new transport facilities they offer (for now Brindisi is linked by road to Bordeaux) are completely changing the sociological and commercial picture of Provence — at least, this Languedocien part of it. The Marseille-Fos area is a desert devoted to oil refineries, while the north is steadily being turned into a tourist area which echoes the Côte d'Azur. The heart of Provence still beats, but in somewhat beleaguered fashion, between these two great options which are rendering life more urban and less rural. A new and specious cosmopolitanism is being born.

The tree-lined boulevards extend from the ruined Roman ramparts in hesitant fashion, as if suffering from loss of memory — imperial memory! It is inside this loop that the nucleus of the modern town still exists — tortuous, narrow, ill-paved streets, badly lighted at night, and since the Algerian war full of North African children replacing the vanished gypsies who have been pushed a little to the south towards the Saintes. Here the mistral prowls and leaves a layer of thick dust on hats and windowsills, on the windscreens of cars, on café tables and their glasses. But in its humble way a little square shelters the heartbeat of modern Provence, for it is here that one finds the statue of the poet Mistral. The Place du Forum used to be called Place des Hommes — a laconic name which signified that here people in search of land-jobs — farmhands and bailiffs and the like — came in search of an employer. You can imagine yourself walking about the Roman forum of such a town in the character perhaps of a Greek *négociant* of olive oil — Plato the philosopher was such a businessman in private life! Very much at home, then, in a spacious forum which was the civic centre, the commercial heart of the town. It was enfiladed with cool porticoes, each with its different function; here a man came to read the news, the official proclamations which were posted up by the town crier. Here, too, one could listen to political orators trying out their political themes against forthcoming elections. Or just stroll about and greet old friends with gossip to exchange. Here the ladies went about their shopping at the little stalls or the artisans' booths, or in the market for fruit and meat and vegetables brilliant under cool awnings. On some days there was a flourishing slave-market, while grouped about the central forum buildings were others like the curial (the administrative centre), the bourse (the municipal treasury), the public granaries, the prison, the temples and the law courts . . . As for the official statue of Mistral, time and circumstances have sanctified it. It is no aesthetic triumph, nor did the poet himself care for it much, but it is difficult not to accord it an affectionate glance. It is true that with his pointed beard and broad-brimmed hat he much resembles his friend Buffalo Bill, whose visit to Provence was such a success that echoes of it can be heard even today.

Buffalo Bill arrived in Europe with a whole rodeo and gave a series of Wild West performances in several countries; the most successful and the most unlucky was the Naples rodeo when somebody stole all the takings. In Provence he fared better, and very particularly in the bull-worshipping Camargue with its little palaeolithic bulls and its long personal tradition of bull-dusting and cockade-snatching. Even the traditional costume was a subtle blend of Spanish panache and French stylishness which quite won the American's heart. You may still gaze upon his pistols, proudly displayed in the *mairie* of Albaron; as for Mistral, his friendship with the great American cavalier was warm and genuine. When he left, Mistral was given a dog as a present, and if you should visit the little cemetery where the poet lies buried, in Maillane, you will find a sculpted portrait of the canine pet on his tomb.

As one crosses the little square on the way to the old Forum, little of which now exists, you will find your breath snatched away by a sudden, almost accidental glimpse of something more grandiose still and more apposite to the Roman experience, the magnificent amphitheatre, less well preserved than that of Nîmes, but better oriented. It is also the largest in the whole of France, rising gigantically against the blue, gem-like sky. It is 500 yards in circumference, with two storeys of sixty arches, the lower Doric and the upper Corinthian — they blend with no feeling of incongruity. It was once picked out with small towers but the coping has crumbled and the whole edifice has a somewhat forlorn and ruined appearance. But nothing can lessen the splendour of the construction. One can wander among the five massive corridors which give on to the forty-three tiers of seats which in the days of Arles' greatness could give place to 30,000 spectators. As for the somewhat out-of-place towers, they appear to date from the eighth century and to be of Saracenic provenance. They detract from the massive beauty of the building. But they remind one that both this amphitheatre and that of Nîmes were at one time turned into fortresses in order to withstand sieges. (The same fate befell Vespasian's Colosseum in Rome at a different date.)

The bigger amphitheatre served for the public games mostly in the form of combats between wild animals and armed gladiators, but the theatres played a humbler but intimate civic role when one thinks that they accommodated all kinds of literary and political gatherings, not to mention musical. It was a world which amused itself with poetry and rhetoric, with sophistry and declamation, with ideas . . . But on the more popular plane, the theatre might offer you public competitions, lotteries, distribution of bread or oil gifted by some pious elder citizen to aid the poor. Not to mention foreign jugglers and monitors of dancing bears from the other wing of the vast Empire, men who hardly spoke Greek or Latin, from remote corners like Pontus and the Euxine Sea. A public which was large and various was not necessarily too choosy and you could always gather an audience for rope-dancers or Indian jugglers, sword-swallowers, marionette workers, and even cock-fights. But the basic fare was of course the comedies and tragedies of the ancient world. Up to about 100 BC the actors were bewigged in an illustrative fashion. The form and colour of the wig varied according to the personage to be represented; afterwards masks came in, fashioned in pasteboard and stylized to indicate the nature of the character on stage. On the role of the theatre in the Roman and Greek world much remains to be said, but the visitor to Provence will doubtless be struck with amazement at the brilliance of the acoustic engineering even in these half-destroyed edifices where, during his summer holiday, he may hear a concert or see a dramatic performance at Nîmes or Orange. The modern sound engineer working for films (I once spent a summer filming in and around Provence) finds much to astonish him in architecture which was designed to husband sound and to distribute it evenly to large audiences. Not only sound, movement as well, for it has been calculated that the 20,000 spectators who fill the Nîmes arenas today for a Spanish bullfight, can empty this vast building in five minutes without jostling or crowding or pushing. The Roman engineers knew their job, and Provincia drew the benefit of their talents.

If the traveller is lucky enough to get permission to climb the highest tower of the Basilique de Ste-Marie Majeure, he will be rewarded with a magnificent view of the little town and of the fabulous country beyond. A view across the barren Crau towards the far off Alps, upwards towards Beaucaire and Tarascon and downwards towards Marseille and the Mediterranean. These wonderful and variegated plains cover

a large area of some 75 square miles, bounded by the Rhône
on the west, by the Alpilles on the north and by far-reaching
lagoons and estuaries on the east. In the south glimmers the
blue Mediterranean. The Crau is covered — apart from its
alluvial clays and other deposits — with fine shingle apparently ferried down from the Alpine glaciers by the Rhône.

Arlésienne

Opening a corrida thus
Seven black beauties
Riding side-saddle proudly
Among our Roman ruins
Fresh from the Courts of Human Love.
Their lovely hair a simple nest
For violets and lace,
The smart little cap à pie
And when you see the
Galloping swerve of these
Human rainbows you realize
How nothing is really dead
    But
Everything just thinks and waits and knows.
    Yes but
Why or what or for whom?
    Surely
For the black Iberian sacrificial
Bulls, thunderbolts of pure sensation.
They await the cruel preaching steel.
Their blood will smoke in the dust
Predestined for catastrophe they lounge
In darkness wait for the female sword.

But it is the famous women of Arles who keep the town's reputation alive, with their raven hair and flashing looks. The highly becoming national costume they affect is, alas, dying out under the pressure of supermarket values, but there are still many who respect traditional wear as characteristic as the Scots' kilt, and which sets off their natural graces so admirably. It consists of a black dress and shawl with a full white muslin stomacher, plus a very small lace cap on the back of the head bound around with a strip of broad black velvet or a ribbon fastened with gold or jewelled pins.

Among those who have left us good travel books about Provence is, surprisingly, Alexandre Dumas. (It is a pity it has not been translated.) It is lively and wide awake. Of the girls of Arles he notes:

"Their reputation for beauty is completely justified, and is something more than just beauty. They are both gracious in demeanour and of a great distinction. Their features are of the greatest delicacy and of a Grecian type; for the most part they have dark hair and black velvety eyes such as I have only seen hitherto in Indians or in Arabs. Yet from time to time in the middle of a typically Ionian group you will see passing a young woman of a Saracen cast of feature with eyes of a longish sort with turned-up corners; she is of olive colouring, with youthful breasts and a child's feet. Or else you may glimpse a tall girl of Gaulish extraction with blonde hair and blue eyes and a walk which is both grave and calm."

This literary snapshot was taken in the 1830s but the same scene presents itself today, only in a slightly more diluted form. The spirit of the people, however, remains constant in its vivacity and intelligence. And despite the ruined state of the monuments it remains outstanding in its beauty and sadness.

The beauties of the new town comfortably matched the

prodigious luxury of the Arles markets of which Honorius and Theodosius in the fifth century have left us the following note: "Everything that the Orient could dream up, or perfume-haunting Arabia or luxury-loving Assyria, or Africa's fertile soils provide, not to mention the productions of lovely Spain and flowering Gaul — all of this is to be found in Arles in the same quantity as in its land of origin."

The abundant fresh water enabled the place to think in terms of public baths and fountains on a handsome scale, while the drainage system had a diameter of 3.50 metres, and the public latrines had running water and were all in white marble. You will think enviously of these aspects of the imperial past of Arles if ever you should be taken short there, for the modern Frenchman seems relatively indifferent to creature comforts. This serves to emphasize how seedy and run-down this little jewel of a town has become. It never really recovered from the invasions by barbarians of one sort or another, chiefly Saracens, though in AD 400 it actually became the capital of Gaul, as it was then constituted, and enjoyed a second period of fame, stability and progress.

In the Middle Ages Arles was ravaged by Visigoths, but in AD 879 was lucky enough to become the capital of a kingdom which lasted 255 years and was governed by eleven kings; then the reins of office passed to consuls. In the succeeding eighty-nine years there were alternations of royalty with republic until the year 1220, when a modest podestat was established. The rest of its history is uneventful — one of neglect, mismanagement, slow ruin setting in. Only the prospect of coining some money out of tourism has caused a factitious revival of interest in splendid ruins like these, and governments are actually beginning to spend money on restoration work as part of the tourist budget. There are only a few real treasures of ancient architecture left in Arles — it has suffered terribly from the repeated vandalism inflicted by conquering armies — and they are all graphic ruins of different ages, for the most part best seen at sunset or by moonlight; the shadow will disguise their pitiful shortcomings in stone, so often have they been used as a quarry for other edifices. Of the theatre, built under Augustus, hardly a stitch is left in terms of the original. It doesn't somehow matter, for the site is infinitely touching and nostalgic in its beauty. Apart from the fine museums, I must not forget to indicate the presence of two jewels of the Romanesque. I am thinking of the unique cloisters of the church of St-Trophime, as well as the marvellously intricate decorations for the great portals which are the purest music of the carver's skill. But these will tend to group themselves in the tourist's mind with the equally glorious façade of the St-Gilles church, which shares its celebrity. Those who wish to savour the atmosphere of the modern town and its inhabitants will take time off to have a cigarette and a drink in the famous Boulevard des Lices with its wide pavements and comfortable cafés, its shady corners sheltered by tall planes with their dappled leaves. Or wander at twilight down the evocative avenues of the Alyscamps, that vast necropolis which is today perhaps the most poetic corner of Arles, nestling in the shadows cast by its knotted parasol pines and oaks. For my money this is the most graphically beautiful place in Arles, and the most atmospheric. This extraordinary necropolis is a spot so shady and delightful that it compels the imagination even though one walks down avenues lined with stone sarcophagi. It radiates harmony and peace, unlike most modern cemeteries, and is an ideal spot for a picnic, with its green lawns shaded by trees and littered with tombs. Although the vast Christian and pagan burial grounds were once separated, the area has gradually contracted as the centuries passed, and there are some parts which have been reclaimed by nature, by ploughed fields and vineyards, and some indeed by treasure hunters and archaeologists. The crosses and sarcophagi which once abounded have for the most part been removed to the town museum (remarkable for its size and the variety of its treasures). But a very great number of the stones have been used decoratively to line the famous "Avenue of Tombs," and this is the walk which is so full of atmosphere, in its dignity and calm restfulness, that one is tempted to feel that here, at last, one can fully realize what it was like to be a Roman resident of old Provence. The Alyscamps offers one a unique experience, and it is worth making time for it, setting aside a whole afternoon and evening to study its variegated beauties. One could not plead in such terms for the Palace of Constantine, though its interest is compelling in the historic sense — for it has been inhabited by Visigoth, Ostrogoth and Frankish kings in turn, as well as the Emperors of Germany when they came down here to crown the Kings of Arles. Lastly, too, by the Comtes de Provence . . . But let us leave history to the histories which have been admirably compiled. This account is necessarily partial and particular rather than comprehensive; it is an attempt to deal with echoes and atmospheres.

At the entry to the Alyscamps is the Arc de St-Césaire which somehow sets the tone for the necropolis beyond. Here reigns a sort of death-in-life. The Elysian fields of Arles are of great antiquity and have had an extraordinary history (Ariosto mentioned them in *Orlando Furioso*, while Dante speaks of them in the *Inferno*), parts of the cemetery serving at one time or another for both Christian and pagan burials. The gradual disintegration of the pagan world, the replacement of polytheism, with its rich tapestry of nymphs and goddesses and other deities, by the more rigidly functional monotheism of the Judaeo-Christian style, was a slow business. You can follow out its history through the long list of bishops and other religious worthies who figure in the history of the town. They are not all of equal interest, though some of the stories about the miracles they caused are richly fanciful and not without humour. But for our purposes one or two are interesting. St Virgil of Arles consecrated Augustine for his mission to Kent, to bring the good news to the Angles. The other figure of note is no less than St Trophimus, who brought Christianity to Arles. Said now to be a Greek — or at least an Asiatic — and to be the apostle who accompanied St Paul, he is mentioned in Acts xx:4. As a relic of pagan times, the Alyscamps remained intact owing to the belief that Christ himself appeared while St Trophimus was consecrating and appropriating it for Christian burial: Christ knelt to bless the spot and you may still see the marks left by his knees in the rock. A little chapel has been built around the sacred spot which is known, appropriately enough, as La Genouillade (built 1529).

For a long time it was the most coveted burial ground for Christians in all Europe. It was enough to float a corpse down the Rhône in its coffin: wrapped in a winding sheet and with the price of burial placed in its mouth, it drifted slowly down to a point opposite Trinquetaille where a group of river-people waited to pull it ashore and carry it to the Alyscamps for formal burial. This convention held good for centuries, and the richness of the decoration on the stone sarcophagi was proverbial.

Its reputation, however, began to wane after the body of St Trophimus was removed in 1152. As for the monolithic tombs, they were abandoned to anyone who cared to have them and for many centuries have been regarded as stone ready to be quarried for use. The town officials fell into bad ways, such as offering the beautifully carved stone sarcophagus lids as civic gifts to distinguished visitors! I am reminded of a passage in Lenthéric which is worth quoting in full — it concerns the plundering of the Alyscamps.

"All the museums of the south of France possess tombs stolen from the Alyscamps . . . The city of Arles has on several occasions had the culpable condescension of giving up the tombs of its ancestors to the princes and great men of the world: Charles IX loaded several ships with them — which sank in the Rhône at Pont-St-Esprit. The Duke of Savoy, the Prince of Lorraine, the Cardinal Richelieu and a hundred others have taken away just what they liked, and Arles today has hardly more to show of this vast cemetery than one avenue — but a noble one — of sarcophagi and some fragments of five Gothic or Romanesque chapels lost in the midst of a desert."

The little town we see today is no doubt also a victim of the railway which has shouldered its way right through the centre. So long as navigation on the great river was a reality, the native economy flourished; but the *coup de grâce* was the establishment of the railway which put in an appearance in 1848 and swallowed up a large corner of this magical ancient burial-place — its goods department even bit off a piece of the Alyscamps. It is so strange when one is sitting among the tombs, drinking in the vast melancholy and resignation of this great burial ground, perhaps the most celebrated Christian cemetery in Europe, to hear a shriek as a train passes through the screen of trees and out of sight beyond, scarcely a hundred yards away. But even the part that escaped has a wonderful valedictory atmosphere, and I have had the luck to visit it on numerous occasions at differing times of year. It never changes, even though it has so obviously been pillaged of its noblest tombs. It is unique in its charm.

Yet despite this calamitous catalogue of misadventures Arles still bears itself proudly, still glows with life. The atmosphere is unique, the evening silence echoing with owls. The river grazes it, and looking across one can see the shady purlieus of Trinquetaille, not to mention other Rabelaisian corners rendered famous by his allusions to them in his book (Bombe-Cul is one!).

At the far end of the owl-haunted garden of tombs rises

the shadowy precinct of St-Honorat. It is much ruined and defaced yet somehow evocative in its echoing vastness. In the eleventh century some attempt was made to take the ruin in hand and rebuild it in the Romanesque style; it was not carried through to a finish. However, the two-stage octagonal tower of Romanesque inspiration gives it coherence, and the general disposition of the trees which surround it give it eloquence and sweetness which is time-defying. *Memento mori!* Even death in this hallowed corner of France seems of good disposition, to be a pleasant mortgage upon a Provençal immortality.

The Rhône at Beaucaire

Precision of a new day lifting through vines
To reflect its blue, the shameless pretext
Of its flowing water like a slang
The priapism of the jungle gone to seed,
Witty with promise of harvests to come
The poet's great laboratory and creed
The word which flows on stanchless as human need,
Or the river, rhythms of memory traced in the blood
So graphic yet so untranslatable to others:
Your beauty, Françoise, the Rhône at Beaucaire.

– VII –

The Story of Marius

If history were always just, a book about Provence could
hardly help but begin with the Roman general Marius, whose
fame has dwindled with time in favour of that of Julius Caesar,
who now overshadows the imagination of the present —
somewhat unjustly, I always feel, when I think of the importance of the classic campaign that Marius mounted and
fought: of its vast significance. Of course in his own day
Marius was just as widely celebrated: to judge by the funerary
inscriptions on the thousands of Gallo-Roman tombs we have
inherited, you might suppose that almost every other male
child was named after him in Provence. And his name has
passed into modern folklore of the Marcel Pagnol period —
the comedians Marius and Olive are held to exemplify the
rustic wit and conversational salt of the Midi. It is perhaps a
somewhat singular sort of immortality for someone who was
once worshipped almost as a god for having saved the civilized world from ruin, yet it has a kind of moral justice for it
shows that this tough little Roman soldier lives on in the heart
of contemporary legend, in the hearts of the people. And the
tactical brilliance of his beautifully orchestrated campaign
against the invading Teutons and the Cimbri might indeed
be said to have saved civilization: it was as great as anything

Caesar performed in later times, though the guides deal with the matter in somewhat perfunctory fashion. Shortage of space must explain it because the little green Michelins are above all reproach in their composition and editorial skill. But in a winter of reading our Romans we found increasingly that the great figure of Caius Marius over-shadowed the early history of the land. It seemed untruthful not to accord him his rightful place as the guardian angel of Roman Provence, so with Aldo I set about cobbling a potted history of his career from my Plutarch and Tacitus — something which would situate his campaign in context as one of the great decisive battles of world history. If Marius had failed . . . but the idea would have made a European's blood run cold, for what was at stake was the whole Roman Empire — civilization!

In or around the year 113 BC there appeared on the right bank of the Danube, to the north of the Adriatic, a vast horde of Nordic "barbarians" which set about ravaging Noricum (ancient Austria) and initiating a grave threat to the borders of Italy. Despite their great numbers two tribes prevailed, the Cimbri (*Kaempir* or warriors) and Teutons (i.e. pure German stock). But they were not simply a horde of destructive marauders hunting for loot. In a sense it was more serious, for they were refugees on the run. They had been dispossessed of their homelands in the Cimbric peninsula by calamitous floods, both of the rivers and the sea. (They inhabited a region which was later to be called Jutland and Holstein.) They were trying to emigrate to more hospitable lands — whole communities with wives and children and domestic livestock. They had all their worldly goods with them in carts covered rudely with ox-skins. It may well be imagined that their anxiety and fatigue had put them in an ugly mood. Nor was their initial reception very encouraging, for the Romans behaved haughtily; it is clear, from their contemptuous refusal to allow the barbarians to settle, that they underestimated the threat to Italy. The barbarians themselves were also

somewhat irresolute, wandering about the central areas of
Germany but moving steadily southward. Papirius Carbo,
consul, was dispatched to deal with the main body. He treach-
erously attacked them and much to his surprise and annoy-
ance was smartly defeated — for after all it was an army with
which he had to deal, and made up of seasoned warriors.
However, for the moment the hordes did not venture to cross
the Alps, they flowed west into the Swiss valleys, sweeping
up other races and tribes by the hungry momentum of their
advance. Amongst them the Ambrons, a German race,
swelled the ranks of the fighting units. Their great numbers
gave them courage and in 110 BC they burst into Gaul together
and reached the Rhône, thus menacing the Roman province.
But their fear and respect for the Roman might made them
hesitate. They applied once more to be granted lands on
which to settle but Silanus the Roman governor, obviously
an idiot, answered insultingly that the commonwealth had
neither lands to distribute nor services to accept from mere
barbarians. Instead he attacked them and was summarily defeated. Things were getting more serious and this time Rome
sent in three consuls with all the levies she could collect to
mount a serious attack on the unwelcome newcomers. But
here an unexpected breakdown in Roman morale took place,
for the gigantic stature of the Nordics, their wild looks and
their fearful cries and screams as they worked themselves up
to fever pitch for battle, struck the Roman troops dumb with
terror. They had never seen anything like this — one imagines they were mostly unblooded levies or local regiments,
and not the regular army. At all events the catastrophe was
total; the barbarians moved in for the kill and the result of
the battle was that some 200,000 Romans were slaughtered.
It was an unheard-of setback for Roman *amour-propre*. As for
the barbarians, their victory gave them confidence, it bred
presumption. The chieftains called a meeting to deliberate
whether they should not cross into Italy forthwith to enslave

or exterminate the Romans. Scaurus, a Roman prisoner who spoke their language, was present at these deliberations and laughed them to scorn, saying, "By all means go, but you will find the Romans invincible." In a transport of fury one of the chiefs present ran him through with his sword. Nevertheless the warning had some effect; the barbarian forces scoured the province but did not yet dare to invade the sacred soil of the peninsula. But for how long . . . ?

Now the Cimbri broke away from the main body and passed into Spain on a prolonged reconnaissance, tempted by the prospects of loot. After fairly ravaging the country they hurried back and reunited with the other tribes, which by now had resolved to hesitate no longer but to advance into Italy on a double front; their swollen numbers allowed them this strategy. The Cimbri were to advance through the Brenner Pass and the Adige while the Teutons and Ambrons were to cross by the Maritime Alps.

It did not take long to get this vast army on the move and the utmost terror prevailed in Rome, and indeed throughout Italy and Provence as well. At last the true proportions of the danger were revealed and by common consent there was only one man who might possibly deal with it in decisive fashion. This was Marius, who, though of lowly birth, was already illustrious and esteemed by the senate for his military genius which had already given him a number of successes in the field. Though plebeian by birth there was no gainsaying his talent. And the people loved him and saw him as one of themselves. Moreover the army feared and loved him for his personal bravery and belief in rigorous discipline. He was a stern, rugged little man lacking education, eloquence and riches, but dextrous and resolute in the field and with an innate tactical gift. His father had been a farmer and Marius's hands had been made hard by his work at the plough. As a free-born Latin he had been called to serve in the wars and had rapidly distinguished himself.

Provence

He was consul in Africa when he was called upon to address himself to the problem of the barbarian hordes. On reaching Provence he found the Roman forces hopelessly demoralized by their disaster, and discipline woefully relaxed. He set about remedying matters, aware that the presence of a general famous for his courage and resolution would act like a tonic on the battle-weary regiments with which he had to deal. Luckily the barbarians, elated and surprised by their unexpected successes as they were, were still somewhat slow to plan a definitive course of action. They still had the Rhône between them and continental Italy and winter was beginning. Traditionally, once they had selected their winter quarters, their forces would be immobilized until the next spring; this military convention was a lucky thing for the Romans as there was still a great deal of doubt and heart-searching about the recent catastrophic defeat. It was clear that the main problem was not simply logistical but really psychological, and it required a delicacy of appreciation which must have dictated to Marius the outlines of his forthcoming strategy. In view of the critical importance of the imminent encounter it was blindingly clear that he could not risk another panic, another breakdown in Roman morale. He must see to it that his regiments of the line familiarized themselves with the gigantic stature of their blood adversaries, and managed to surmount their fear of Teutons and Ambrons alike. He resolved to deal gingerly with the barbarian forces, to haunt and shadow them without risking a major confrontation until he could draw them into battle on his own terms, and on a field of his choice. But the Romans must set about familiarizing themselves with them, for familiarity would breed contempt and revive a disposition to discipline. I hope I have not given the impression of an unimaginative if rugged little disciplinarian, someone lacking in fantasy; it is clear that Marius did not lack insight. There is a note in Plutarch which makes him sound someone of character, or at any rate a man of superstitions, for "he had with him, apart from his wife Julia, a Syrian woman named Martha who was said to have the gift of prophecy. She was carried about in a litter with great solemnity, and the sacrifices which he offered were all supervised under her direction. When she assisted at such sacrifices she wore a double purple robe, while in her hand she held a ceremonial spear adorned with ribbons and garlands." Dare one imagine that Marius depended on her for advice on military matters as well as predictions based on second sight? It is not impossible. At any rate his tactical appreciation of the state of things showed vision and experience and in the long run bore the desired fruit. But for the time being the basic thing was to let his troops get used to these blond giants with their wild looks and savage cries. He set himself to shadow them without offering an engagement.

By now of course all the inhabitants of Arles, Tarascon, Glanum, Cavaillon — indeed all the Graeco-Gaulish townships — had taken to the hills. The Alpilles still offered limestone hills as protection, for the barbarians were much hampered by the chain of interlinking lagoons which they must cross to achieve a definitive southward penetration. Water — too much or too little — was still a great problem in this land of lagoons.

The central plain (not unlike the Attic plain) is still today much as it was then, and the tourist who selects the flock of towns which border it, say, Arles, Nîmes, Glanum, Tarascon, Orange, Aix, will rapidly become aware of Marius's problems. Apart from the great fast-flowing rivers like the Rhône and Durance (the only crossings then were fords which were often flooded) the central flats were also exasperatingly capricious once the autumn rains began. A network of interlocking lagoons and lakes scribbled the whole verdant surface, with the overflow of rivers always advancing and receding, their levels always changing. The traveller then with any knowledge of the state of things was apt to stick to the slightly higher land of the Alpilles. This is what Marius elected to do. He allowed the invading army to cross the Rhône without molestation so that they had the wide river at their backs, but he stuck to the higher land while the barbarians tended to follow the path of least resistance (out of ignorance) and to flow into the central plain which was broad enough to let them deploy their forces; only to find, however, that they must advance very much on tiptoe because of the lagoons and the marshes. From the encircling chain of hills the army of Marius shadowed them, marching along the parallel paths which led towards Aix, where a major bifur-cation of what was later the Via Aurelia led away southward into Italy. But while his troops were getting used to the bar-barian presence the little general did not waste his time; he established a strong camp at Ernaginum, now St-Gabriel, at the extreme limit of the Alpilles to the west. Then he set his men to dig a strategic canal to link up the lagoons below, opening a mouth into the sea through the Etang de Galejon so that if necessary he could be victualled by ship.

So matters stood during the short winter season; but in the spring of 102 BC, when the grass had grown sufficiently to feed their horses and their domestic animals, the Teutons and the Ambrons packed their tents and struck camp, their forces forming up with the intention of continuing their advance. Plutarch says:

"They soon appeared in immense numbers, with their hid-eous looks and wild cries, drawing up their chariots and planting their tents in front of the Roman camp. They show-ered upon Marius and his soldiers continual insult and de-fiance. So much so that the Romans in their irritation would fain have rushed out of their camp to engage them but Marius was not to be drawn and he dissuaded them. 'It is no question of gaining triumphs and trophies,' he said, with his rough convincing logic, 'but literally averting the storm of war and saving Italy.' "

One day a Teuton chieftain came up to the very gates of the camp and called out to Marius. He challenged him to hand-to-hand combat, but Marius was not to be drawn. He had the huge ogre of a man informed by an interpreter that if he was tired of life nothing prevented him from hanging himself! But the excited barbarian kept on insisting, so the general sent him down a gladiator. However, he made his troops mount guard upon the ramparts in regular succession to get them familiarized with the cries, weapons and appearance of the barbarians. The most distinguished of his officers, young Serorius, whose tragic history is itself a romance, and who understood and spoke Gallic well, penetrated in disguise into the camp of the Ambrons; he kept his chief informed of what was going on there. At last the barbarians, in their impatience at having vainly tried to provoke the Romans to leave their camp, struck their own and put themselves in motion once more towards the Alps. Marius followed them along the scarps, observant of their every movement but still refusing a definitive engagement.

So they reached Orgon. There the limestone precipices rise as walls sheer above the plain, now crowned by a church and a couple of ruined castles. It was probably from this point that the general watched the barbarian hordes defile past. For six whole days, says Plutarch, the invading hordes flowed before the Roman positions. The Teutons, gazing at the Roman legionaries watching them motionless from the high cliffs, flung at them a taunting question: "Have you any messages for your wives in Italy? We shall soon be with them!"

The restive soldiers, still restrained by Marius, waited until the whole horde had passed, and then the general gave the order to strike camp and follow. Crossing the dip at Lamanon, probably where the overspill of the Durance had once carried its rolled and polished stones into the barren plain of the Crau, the Roman force regained the heights on the further side of the Touloubre, at Pélissanne. Still hugging the high ground, he at last came up with the barbarians at Les Milles, which is about 4 miles to the south of Aix. The whole pattern of his strategy was beginning to unfold according to plan, for he was coaxing them into a position from which it would be possible to launch a decisive attack on the main body, provided his veteran force had overcome any misgivings about the size of their adversaries. He had kept a sharp eye on the foe, and had seen that the Ambrons had detached themselves from the main body near Aix and were now directing their attention to Marseille. At Les Milles the red sandstone cliffs stand above the river Arc which makes a broad clean sweep, leaving a green meadow in the loop.

It was a delectable spot, for countless interlacing springs, some of them boiling hot and some cold, flowed from under the rocks into natural cauldrons and baths of natural stone; they have mostly disappeared since the time of Marius, indeed all the hot springs, which gave such delight to the Romans and made the reputation of places like Nîmes as health-giving spas during the days of the Empire, have suffered a steep decline in temperature.

Here Marius pitched on a place for his camp which, while unexceptionable in point of strength, afforded little water. But when his soldiers complained of thirst he pointed to the river which flowed by the enemy camp and told them that they would have to purchase their water with their blood. This caused some murmuring, and they said: "Why then do you not lead us there before our own blood is quite parched?" He replied, more mildly, "I will; but all in good time. First let us fortify our camp."

He was still occupied with his central psychological problem of morale; he really wanted to blood his legionaries, to give them a taste of the enemy's blood and see how they reacted. Had they got over their trauma or not? Here a fortuitous skirmish provided the answer he sought, for while the soldiers obeyed orders the problem of water fuelled the impatience of the camp followers who needed to water their animals, horses and cattle. They decided to force the issue and take what they needed. They ran in crowds down the hill to the river, some with pick-axes as well as their buckets and other utensils; others took their swords and javelins. They encountered at first only a small body of the enemy, for the main force was busy bathing in the hot baths and resting as they dined. Tired and travel-worn as they were, they had been quite carried away by the luxurious baths and the delectable landscape into which they had wandered unwittingly. They were not prepared for a Roman attack and were slow in calling up a defence force. The camp followers made no bones about the matter and cut down a number of defenceless barbarians as they were bathing. Their cries brought others to their assistance and the skirmish grew in size. Marius could no longer contain the impetuosity of his soldiers who were uneasy now about the fate of their servants. The engagement grew general — and now Marius had the response to his unspoken question. The Roman legionaries surged down upon the invaders with a violence that left no doubt about Roman determination. They were cured of their misgivings about barbarian physique. Moreover, the forces facing them were the Ambrons who had inflicted the initial defeat on the Roman army, had caused the collapse of Roman might as exemplified by the two consuls Manlius and Caepio who had been sent to defend the frontier. The hated Ambrons who had been taunting them for cowardice for so long! This time they did not stand a chance even though they poured across the river with great resolution shouting their rallying cry "Ambra! Ambra!" The engagement grew bloody and ended in a decisive victory for the Romans. In no time the idyllic little river Arc was choked with barbarian bodies; but the Romans, whose blood was up, pursued those who escaped down the hill right into their own camp. There the women made a desperate resistance, snatching up arms wherever they could, or pouncing on the attackers with naked hands, to catch at their swords, suffering themselves to be hacked to pieces rather than surrender. It was a costly though brief encounter but it gave Marius the signal he awaited. He could now envisage a definitive battle. Nevertheless the Romans spent a slightly anxious night after darkness fell, for though they had defeated their foes and overrun their camp, even they had not time to complete the fortification of their own positions; they dreaded a night attack with the combined forces of Ambrons and Teutons. Fortunately this did not materialize. "A crying was heard from the defeated Ambrons all through the night, not like the sighs and groans of men but like the howling and bellowing of wild beasts."

The decisive Roman victory was still two nights away; the Teutons had obligingly separated themselves from their defeated allies the Ambrons, and it was consequently possible to mount a separate decisive attack upon them. The account in Plutarch is a trifle confused: though he does mention the two battles all right, he writes in ignorance of the actual sites, which are worth studying on the spot. It also has a bearing on the tactics of Marius, for now he was confident enough to detach a force of 3,000 men under Claudius Marcellus, whose job was to climb the long valley to the north of Mont Ste-Victoire, and to fall upon the rear of the enemy once the general engagement developed. The whole strategy worked like a charm. The Teutons and Ambrons, attacked on two fronts simultaneously, now began to realize they had been coaxed into a trap. They fought like demons, but all in vain. The Roman army carried the day. Apparently a fearful carnage ensued. No quarter was given, women and children alike were all mowed down; even the dogs furiously defending their masters' bodies were cut to pieces. Defeat was total and crushing.

After the battle Marius selected from among the captured arms and other spoils of war such as were elegant and entire and likely to make the most striking show in his triumph. The rest he had piled together in a great heap. He proposed to offer them up as a splendid sacrifice to the gods. The army stood around the hillock crowned with laurel while he himself, arrayed in a purple robe, girt after the manner of the Romans, held a lighted torch. He had just raised it with both hands towards heaven and prepared to set fire to the sacrificial pile when some messengers came in sight galloping with all speed towards them, causing a great hush of silence and expectation. The new arrivals were Romans and they leaped from their horses and saluted him with the title of Consul for the fifth time, presenting him with letters to the same purport. This added a note of joy to the solemnity, and the soldiery responded to the news with acclamations and the clanking of small arms; then, while the senior officers were presenting Marius with fresh crowns of laurel, he set fire to the pile and completed the sacrifice.

Accounts differ as to the number of dead and enslaved. Some say that 200,000 of the barbarians were killed and 80,000 made prisoner. The most modest version, however, speaks of 100,000 dead. At all events the slaughter was very great and the corpses appear to have stayed where they fell in default of burial. According to Plutarch they remained rotting in the summer heat and the pestilential battlefield, because of the stench, got the name of Campi Putridi or Fields of Putrefaction, a name perhaps still traceable in that of a neighbouring village, Pourrières.

On the site of this great battle on the south bank of the river, over against the barbarian camp — where also was the ceremonial pyre in which the wagons, chariots, arms and costumes of the invaders were consumed — a monument to

Marius was erected which remained in tolerably good shape, to judge by old engravings of the region, until just before the French Revolution. Later it was just a jumble of ruins, without coherence. It seems to have consisted of a quadrangular block of masonry measuring 15 feet on each side within an enclosing wall 14 feet distant. This block sustained a pyramid with statues at the angle, as it still figures upon the arms of the Commune (to quote an eyewitness who saw it in 1890). He goes on to add, "Here three or four years ago was found a beautiful statue in Parian marble of the Venus Victrix, unfortunately without a head and arms, but clearly of the best Greek workmanship." The city of Avignon purchased it and it is now one of the ornaments of the city museum. The statue, to my mind, proves that the monument in question was raised by Julius Caesar, as it conveys an indirect compliment to his own family. Venus was the ancestress and protectress of the Julian race, and Caesar perhaps insinuated, if he erected the statue, that the success of Marius was due to her patronage and that of Julius Caesar's aunt, the wife of Marius, quite as much as to the genius in war of Marius himself. We know that the trophies erected to Marius for his Cimbric and Teutonic victories were overthrown by Sulla, and that they were re-erected by Julius Caesar in AD 65.

A visit to the site on a fine day convinces one that there is nothing far-fetched about such suppositions; of course there is little to see, the quiet plain drowses in the burning summer heat. Eagles turn in the dazed blue of the sky. The marshes and dikes throb with the croaking of frogs, while down by the slow-moving river the ground is starred with grape hyacinth and white star of Bethlehem. It is more than 1,900 years since the battle and a diligent searcher can still find the occasional piece of pottery or metal from the great pyre. The silence seems dense and weighted with these ancient souvenirs of war. Nor was this the end of Marius's military career: he was lucky enough to bring off the double option. Having secured Italy's frontiers in the west, he returned to the peninsula only to find that the Cimbri had started to invade from the north-east. He met up with them at a similar site near Vercellae and inflicted a defeat upon them no less absolute than that near Aix.

There is much else we might like to know about Marius which would bring him more fully to life in these pages, but history is never eloquent enough about her children and there are obviously gaps in the story which render this account tantalizingly partial. About the general as a man, for example, we know hardly anything except that Julia his wife seems to have accompanied him on his campaigns; and then there is the funerary inscription found in the Alyscamps which mentions Cornelia the daughter of Marius; it would seem that she also travelled in the company of her father and died in or near Arles. It seems strange that he left her there and did not move her body back to Rome: some scholars have cast a doubt on the authenticity of the inscription because of the bad Latin in which it is written. But where such suppositions do not lack plausibility there should be no diffidence in recording them. Certainly the inscriptions found in the Alyscamps yield a thousand examples of dog-Latin, proving that the average Gallo-Roman of that epoch — not to mention the artisans who carved the inscriptions on the memorial stones — had only a nodding acquaintance with the classical language. Another equally moving example which one should not hesitate to set down in relation to Marius is the strange monument which lies at the bottom of the promontory upon which stand the clustered and telescoped buildings of Les Baux. On the eastward side of the main entrance — it seems to have fallen from the precipice above — stands the erection now known as the Trémaié, a vulgarized version of Les Trois Maries. It consists of a block of limestone about 25 feet high in which, some 12 feet from the ground, is sculpted a semi-circular-headed niche, 5½ by 4½ feet wide, which contains a group of three personages; a bearded man on the left of the observer, a tall woman in the centre wearing a mitre, and on the right a third woman. At first blush one might be forgiven for thinking that the sculpture is mediaeval, but if you climb· on the roof of the little chapel, which has grown up under the ornament, and examine the carving attentively, you will be satisfied that it is work of the classic period, and the figures are dressed in Augustan tunics and togas. Moreover, below the figures is an inscription which is quite unmistakable, though unhappily it can only be partially deciphered:

> . . . F. CALDUS
> . . . AE POSVIT P . . .

The three figures are impressive and indeed moving despite their gnawed appearance. They are life-size and oriented sunwards. It has been surmised with a very great deal of probability that they represented Marius, his wife Julia and the enigmatic Syrian prophetess who accompanied him in his campaign against the Teutons and Ambrons. If this is the case we can understand the name given to the group — and the ensuing muddle over it. For Les Trémaiés must have meant the three Marii, that is to say Caius Marius, Marth Marii and Julia Marii. One might venture a further suggestion — which is not too improbable to entertain — namely, that this was a victory trophy set up on the heights of Les Baux to mark one of the points of vantage from which Marius watched the barbarian horde flow by in the valley beneath him, biding his time! At any rate the Caldus whose name is on the monument was probably Caius Caelius Caldus, one of Marius's lieutenants in the war against the Cimbri. He was created Consul in 97 BC.

Lawrence Durrell

Princess X

A Russian Amazon who bruises minds
And gave me a sore memory blitz
Awakes these graphic lines —
Sometimes insists on looking like
A sick mule, or a mutinous cherub
Cocotte-minute and camisole de force in one,
At others like the down draught
From the furnace of a love-machine,
Cheeky groom that everyone would shun.
She was for me a gorgeous python
In a nightdress of monkeys' skulls.
She ushered death in, the perfect go-between,
Beautiful in her harmony of pearls
She loitered with smiles among her naked girls.
A necklace of rats not all of them dead,
She wrote her poems for the most part in bed.

– VIII –

The Jealous God

The history of Provence, with its slow evolution of the European consciousness, is quite inescapably bound up with such stars of the first magnitude as Caesar and Antony, Marius and Hannibal, swarthy generals who carved up the Roman territories of the epoch in the interests of peace and security — or in the interests of strategic expansion. Among them I have always been astonished by the relatively lowly position occupied by the great Agrippa (Marcus Vipsanius) whose short life (63–12 BC) was so packed with battles as well as public works of great elegance and utility. I suppose it is due to the fact that, almost alone of the great men of the time, he never sought the limelight, was a secretive and quite unselfseeking executive of the monarchy, indeed became the prime agent of Octavian's rise to power and the pillar of the Augustan monarchy in which he is reported to have believed with an almost mystical passion. His relationship with the Emperor was based on the complete trust he inspired as an instrument of the royal will; he was like a creative flirtation of identical selves with one thought in common: the preservation of the *Pax Romana* of the day and the affirmation of the monarchic succession.

The country is littered with fragments of public works of

great magnificence whose inspiration was this great governor, consul, and military captain. It is impossible to contemplate the shattered and spliced fragments of the La Turbie monument without feeling a certain awe at the ambitiousness of the intention — no less than the tragic nature of the outcome, for this huge public work was intended to celebrate the Roman subjugation of the countless tribes and races which together went to make up the Europe of the day. It was intended to glorify Augustus as well as to mark (as in *Alpis summa*) a natural rural division between the two Italys, so to speak. A notice pronounced the fact in no uncertain terms, thus: *Huc usque Italia: abhinc Gallia!* The monument took the form of an elaborate tower with decorative outcrops of statuary and was intended, say some historians, to be as memorable a declaration of faith as was the Pharos which adorned the promontory of Alexandria. Alas for human pride, the subsequent waves of history did not spare it. The barbarian forces rolled back and forth over the area, tearing it down with each advance and retreat. This wretched state of affairs went on until 1705 when it was definitively blown up with explosives. The present ignoble trophy was pasted together with what was left of the statuary!

But you are most likely to feel a sudden keen wave of curiosity and awe about Agrippa if you find yourself standing at sunset upon the great stone plinth of the Pont du Gard, which together with the magnificent Parthenon in Rome is the handiwork of this prodigious and enigmatic personage who has been somewhat passed over by the historians, perhaps because he was not so dramatic and colourful as those with whom he shared the Provençal stage. As a general he was certainly superior to Antony, perhaps even to Caesar: he was with Octavian at Apollonia when the news of Caesar's murder came through, and he accompanied the latter to Rome to claim the succession and the inheritance. From then on Agrippa's destiny allied him to the monarchy. Was he conscious that from this point he had embarked on the steep and dangerous path which power politics always entails? One does not know, for his autobiography has been lost, as has been the geography he is also supposed to have left us on his early death at 51 years of age. What is known of Agrippa projects the portrait of a first-class executive and administrator who could also handle armed forces in the field as well as ships of the line at sea. Octavius adored him and when he came to power he heaped honours on him despite his plebeian origins. It was Octavius who made Agrippa put away his wife and marry his own daughter Julia. Indeed he had children by her, Caius and Lucius, but one died of an infected wound and the other of a decline — possibly a sort of leukaemia. Another son, an ill-conditioned youth, was put to death at the behest of Octavius (the order was given on his death-bed, apparently, to leave no excuse for internecine war). Hazard and violence seem to have dogged his private life. The only bust we have of Agrippa conveys a robust and forthright personality, plain-speaking; one imagines a somewhat squat peasant figure, gracious but shaggy–uncouth. Completely truthful and unselfish in his dealings with politicians and fellow executives, he was unique in the Rome of his day. Moreover, he seems to have been just as happy and absorbed in building some colossal work like the Pont du Gard as in designing and executing the *cloaca maxima* of the new Rome. He was more than just an engineer mesmerized by the functional attributes of his stoneworks: the functional perfection was raised to the rank of aesthetic wonder; his eye was that of a superb artisan with a lust for fine stone and a profound feeling for the stresses engendered by the passage of water in its canals.

But his family history, so fraught with tragedy, must be my excuse for finding his only portrait inexpressibly sad — for sad beyond comparison is the family history of the general who determined the shape of the Roman world by his victory at Actium. His daughter, Agrippina, starved herself to death, heartbroken at the murder of her two sons by Tiberius, and despairing because the only family representative was now the crazy and debauched Caligula. The other daughter of Agrippa, Julia, was hardly less famous (or infamous) for her own excesses. She died in banishment. At this remove the family was represented by the second Agrippina (daughter of the first) who was to become the mother of Nero. Yes, Nero, the son who became the murderer of his mother as well as his brother, and who died at last by his own hand amidst the execrations of the Roman world!

It is difficult to match the portrait of this grave and composed administrator with those other faces which stare out at one from the shadows of Roman history: a gallery of theatrical freaks to illustrate the decadence and ruin of the great empire they ruled. Even Agrippa with his multiple talents, both civil and military, could not halt the pace of its decline. In his various offices and governorships (he ruled Gaul for Rome, he ruled Spain) he naturally accumulated great fortunes, but here again he showed that he was not a grasping man who spent his wealth upon himself. Wherever he found himself *en poste* he spent his money in true Roman fashion, in improving and embellishing the cities over which he had been sent to rule. In the case of Nîmes, however, we have good reason to believe that it was love at first sight, for he planted and decorated and enriched this verdant precinct in quite exemplary fashion. When he found it, it was called Nemausus (the name comes from the Celtic word *naimh*, meaning a fountain or spring). It could not be more appropriate, for the most striking feature of the town today is the spring which wells up in the centre of the garden known as the Jardin de la Fontaine. Under a fertile limestone cliff topped by the now deserted Tour Magne wells up an extravagant arm of noiseless green water: thick, profuse and quite transparent, a flowing sleeve of green jade in whose opaque depths your eyes, when they get accustomed to the reflections, may well discern the votive coins and breast-pins and fragments of metal and tin tossed in by the modern pilgrims to the place, thus setting their seals upon a wish or a superstition, just as the ancient Romans or other pagans did of old with votive coins of gold or silver. This spring was what had made the town famous in the world of healing, almost as famous as Eleusis in the ancient world.

Flooded Nîmes

Goblins in rubber that seem so torpid,
Like Hitler's mother in the last photo
Perched on his breast, only the medals showing.
A love bewitched by the classical fraud of Freud,
The personal neurasthenia refined by death —
Greet the dead with the music of shovels,
Or the cellars of Roman Nîmes full of dead cats
Afloat with giant rats feasting on garbage,
Rats the size of human heads in car parks
Built for the higher tourism and its clients
Floating about in the dark fully dressed
At the wheels of their expensive cars,
The wingbeat of crossed eiderdowns at night
By floodlit garages — A nymph with all her rivets showing
Sweet primate of a summer night farewell.
We'll scold the human heart for loving too well.

Once again, though, one must note that the munificence of Agrippa seems a trifle disproportionate to the little town which so many classical authors pass over without particular notice. Like many centres of healing or spas, it was probably populated largely by the sick — perhaps that is the reason. At any rate he spared no effort to increase its natural amenities; he brought it a direct water supply from two fine springs at a distance of 25 miles from the central fountain of the nymphs in the town. Most of this colossal structure, the Pont du Gard, is still standing and can be climbed; it is quite impossible to describe how glorious it is to watch the sunrise or the sunset from the very top. The water no longer flows, of course, but one can still see the three tiers of massive arches which carried it across the valley of the Gardon at a height of 160 feet. The whole work — its length is 873 feet at the top — could be compared to its advantage with the modern aqueduct that conveys fresh water to the Peyrou of Montpellier; it is more lengthy but an altogether lighter structure. Agrippa's great stone bauble conveys a sort of splendid insolent eloquence which seems to be the hallmark of the Roman remains of Provence and elsewhere. As for the oblations to the nymphs, I find that Suetonius mentioned this pilgrims' habit in his life of Augustus, and it is touching to see that this almost involuntary habit still holds force today, though perhaps with changed intentions, different illnesses. At any rate the famous old fountain still yields a mass of votive objects whenever the municipality has cleaned it out. Nowadays, however, there is a fair percentage of Coca Cola bottle tops among the offerings; this is since the town, among its many summer festivities, has become celebrated for the quality and professionalism of its jazz festivals which are widely attended by the young, both foreign and domestic. But in the past the old fountain of the nymphs has yielded an almost inexhaustible supply of coins — Roman-Gaulish and Gallo-Greek, and all collectors (so Aldo avers) knew that even the briefest visit to Nîmes would enable them to furnish their collections with new specimens usually obtained from the *curés* of the various churches. This was because the peasants who were in the habit of digging up these coins in their fields were dishonest enough to slip them into the offertory bags and plates of a Sunday; in consequence the priests always had a good supply to sell to any ardent collector who had the wit to ask them.

Aldo's own collection, which is rich and choice, was obtained with the help of a scholar curate and is proudly housed in a grandiose old cabinet in the château. There are a number of beautiful and graphic issues of coins in this collection, but none which awakes such echoes as the bronze triumphal medal which Augustus had struck to honour Agrippa after his momentous victory at Actium. It is impossible to overemphasize the importance of this decisive engagement in history, and the Emperor was fully aware of the fact. It gave him further cause to esteem his friend, and the text of the inscription underlines the fact in no uncertain fashion. I was proud to obtain a specimen of this important issue, though my example came not from a *curé* but from an old tramp who traded it for the price of a *canon* — the traditional tumbler of Beaujolais!

I will describe it briefly.* The issuing authority is the Colonia Nemausus, and the central feature consists of the backed heads of the two friends in handsome and dramatic association. Agrippa is on the left and wears a rostral crown accorded him for the success at Actium, while Augustus wears a wreath of laurel, bestowed on him in 27 BC (*ob cives servatos*). The inscription or legend elaborates on this a little, reading thus: IMP (erator) DIVI F (ilius), i.e., *imperator* (general), son of the divine (Julius Caesar). Although perfectly appropriate to the period before he was granted the honorific name of Augustus in 27 BC, the form was nevertheless retained throughout the later issues. The reverse side of the medal is more intriguing, picturing as it does the Egyptian crocodile (Cleopatra) chained to a palm tree to commemorate the successful Egyptian campaigns of Octavian. This motif also appears on silver coins of the Roman state with the added

*Compare the example reproduced on pages iii and 200 (enlarged).

inscription AEGYPTO CAPTA, with a risen sun or moon with cloud forms. (These circular disc forms seem to have some strong mystical significance for the nearby Gallic tribes, though at present their meaning has not been discovered.) It is sufficient to recall, however, that Nîmes and the country round about was bestowed upon the troops who shared the hazards of Octavian's Egyptian manoeuvres; it was customary to bestow bounties of land upon the troops as rewards after a successful campaign. Agrippa probably took an active part in fixing up the amenities of the little town so that the men could find their feet in civil life. I would like to believe that he also took an active hand in finishing off the beautiful arenas as they deserved, but for this I cannot furnish absolute proof. There seems no line of activity which did not involve him. After the voyage of Augustus in 27 BC, when it was decided to submit the country to cadastral survey and scientific mapping, who should they turn to but Agrippa? There is nothing to suggest that he wasn't absolutely delighted by the technical problems involved.

He needed no urging to think big, for was it not Agrippa who was called upon to avenge the calamitous defeat that Octavian suffered at the hands of Sextus Pompeius in 38 BC? In this business, as in everything he did, nothing was left to chance. What was obviously needed was a completely new fleet and army, and in order to train the former he constructed a new harbour on the present Bay of Naples by conflating the two shallow lakes called Lucrinus and Avernus, and remodelling them into a sort of estuary; it is reminiscent of the feats of his ancestor Marius with his network of dikes and canals. It is here that Agrippa trained new crews for his ships and the new infantry he had summoned up, and his precautions were amply repaid by the outcome, for in the following year his forces appeared off Sicily and in two decisive actions utterly defeated the army of Sextus Pompeius and set the seal on his reputation as a general who was easily the equal of

Caesar or Mark Antony. This was soon to be proven, for the uneasy truce which divided the spheres of influence in the Roman world between Octavian and Mark Antony was slowly but surely disintegrating, and justice would have to be done with the sword.

For us in our world these figures which seem so much larger than life have been handed down to us by the historians as splendid cartoons of a vanished reality; the dramatists and poets have lent them a second life which has done nothing to diminish their stature. Rather it has increased our awe of them. But among themselves they must have lived a much easier and more familiar corporate life, fully conscious of each other's little foibles or weaknesses. The sort of tiny but salient details which help Suetonius to colour his portraits must have been common currency to all, since Roman society for all its variety and complexity was not numerically overwhelming, and court gossip, then as now, must have occupied a prime place in the public world. Aldo was so pleased with this conceit that he invented a gossipy Roman historian called Euxinus to whom he attributed this kind of salient invention and who, since he did not exist, could not be held accountable for the gossip he shored up in *The Secret Memorials*. It is he who tells us that Agrippa's eyes were set too close together and that he had recurring fevers caught from a campaign in marshlands, or that Antony had bad teeth, while Caesar had a fatal predilection for shellfish which always brought him out in dreadful skin eruptions . . . As for Cleopatra,

"what might have seemed the fruit of caprice in others was in her a quite involuntary manifestation of her destiny expressing itself. This is what made her formidable, she was as slack as a snake with no preconceived opinion about the nature of good and evil. The only thing she knew about from top to bottom was love! She was an inveterate liar and in consequence an incomparable confederate in love."

"My nimble seraph, will you stop looking
over your shoulder? You make a lot of bonnet
about writing to the great man, 'What shall I
say to such a great artist?' Send him a water-
colour of your private parts. Come to these arms
my perfumed killer whose musk defines the
serpent-killer, let me adore your lovely face
and terrify me into Grace.
   Who knows what the love-god could have meant
By this unholy predicament."

E.M. Forster, in his *Alexandria: a history and guide*, has
adorned a felicitous text with some striking thumbnail portraits of the principal personages; but among them he does
not seem able to stand the character of Octavian whom he
regards as a monster of frigidity and calculation, quite unable
to appreciate the dramatic and unexpected quality of the sudden loving attachment which had grown up between Cleopatra and her Roman. (Neither had really solicited anything
so primordial to happen, for the sky to fall in on them in this
fashion. They felt almost aggrieved!) According to Forster,
Octavian's mind was too commonplace to see in this more
than the elements of a vulgar debauch. "Vice, in his opinion,
should be furtive," he declares. But none the less some of
the credit for the victory at Actium can be accorded to him
for his exemplary handling of the land-troops, though the
decisive blow, which pinned the armies of the lovers to the
lee shore of an unpropitious gulf, came from Agrippa.
Throughout the engagement Octavian's strategy was, as far
as possible, to avoid a decisive locking of horns with the
foreign invaders, and in this policy he was successful, but it
was not enough to manoeuvre and temporize. The decisive
action had to be faced as well, and when it came it was
Agrippa's force that provided it.
   When I was at school it was customary to treat the battle

of Actium as a somewhat mysterious event which ended with
an equally mysterious loss of nerve on the Egyptian side and
a sudden unexpected withdrawal. Cleopatra, we were told,
got an attack of cold feet at the last moment and deserted
her lover who was forced to face Agrippa with a sadly depleted fleet and army and limp back after her for fear of losing
the wealth of the Egyptian treasuries and the power of Egyptian influence. This rather schematic account of the battle has,
however, been greatly modified by the modern historian who
takes a much more balanced and charitable view of Antony's
conduct in the field, and of the Egyptian fleet's precipitate
withdrawal. New evidence has come to light also about the
fleet strengths and dispositions, and owing to the importance
of the battle it is worth giving a brief outline of what really
seems to have happened, if only to vindicate the conduct of
poor Cleopatra. She was trying to break the blockade which
Agrippa had fastened upon the lovers' navies. In vain. The
withdrawal, though successful, was characterized by calamitous losses in naval craft. Agrippa had opened the proceedings with a daring raid on the central supply dump of
Antony's army at Methone in the Peloponnese, while his fleet
with a brilliant reflex lunge had pinned his enemy to the lee
shore of the Ambracian Gulf. It was impossible for Antony
to extricate himself and Cleopatra from this clever trap.

Antony's greatness was as a land-commander. Now in
Agrippa he was to face the only Roman who thoroughly
understood naval strategy. The blockade held firm and the
weeks went by with dead slowness, sharpening towards a
particularly torrid summer which led to impatience and hasty
judgements on the part of Antony. Time, too, seemed to be
turning against the lovers, for the veterans of the land forces
started to desert to Octavian's side, while so many rowers
died of fever that when battle was finally joined, Antony could
only call upon the services of some 230 ships against Octavian's 400. It was essential to try and find a way of breaking

loose from the stranglehold and bursting out of the Ambracian Gulf. But how?

The Ambracian Gulf, on the west coast of Greece, narrows to a strait less than a kilometre wide where it meets the sea. On the northern horn of the strait lie the ruins of Nicopolis, the town Octavian founded after this fruitful encounter, as well as the modern town of Preveza, unhealthy and surrounded with pestilential marshlands. To the south lies the scrubby sandy headland with the trifling remains of a temple to Apollo Actios. Here, in 31 BC, Antony and Cleopatra camped with 120,000 infantry and 12,000 cavalry, a force massed for a decisive intervention in the heartlands of Italy itself. The equivocal factor was this damned blockade which held firm and compromised the sea lanes leading out of the Gulf into the open sea . . .

At this point Antony seriously considered abandoning the fleet and striking directly with the infantry across the mainland to where twice before (at Philippi and Pharsalus) the fate of Rome had been decided. But abandoning the fleet meant abandoning Cleopatra's main contribution to his cause. He decided therefore that the best line of action was to provoke a head-on collision of forces with the hope of battering his way through the blockade with the queen in order to return to Egypt and refit. He would leave instructions for his army to cross Greece under his generals and prepare for a Macedonian campaign under his renewed direction the following spring. Alas for such hopes! What in fact came about was seized upon and distorted by Roman propaganda to show a feckless and un-Roman Antony deserting his fleet and army at the behest of his fickle and treacherous oriental queen who had already been suspected of making overtures to the Emperor behind his back! It was far from the truth, which was that they were making a determined attempt to break out of Agrippa's blockade. True, most of their fleet was captured or destroyed, but, as one naval historian has put it, "to save even sixty ships out of 230 was a creditable achievement for a man embayed on a lee shore and vastly outnumbered." The real disaster struck when Antony's army started marching towards Macedonia but was quickly intercepted by the emissaries of Octavian who offered them favourable terms. These blandishments were difficult to refuse, especially after Agrippa's crushing victory at sea. The army started to melt away. As one can see from the historian Michael Grant's *Cleopatra*, it was not that Antony lost the world in that one battle, nor that he lost it for a woman, but that over the course of a land and sea campaign Octavian prudently avoided an engagement by land while Antony was checked again and again by Agrippa at sea. It was morale that finally deserted the army on that September day, Antony only discovering the awful truth when it at last followed him to Egypt.

The subsequent focus for the historic tragedy shifts to Alexandria now, where a perfectly rational despair was setting in and undermining the resolution of the lovers. It was a logistic despair. Octavian was on their heels with his vast army and fleet virtually intact. How long would it take them to reassemble a comparable force in order to outface it in the field? Just the thought made Antony quail. Moreover, it was clear that at the back of his mind Octavian relished the thought of leading the lovers back as trophies in his triumphal march on his return to Rome. And now the excellence of Agrippa's generalship was not in doubt — he was clearly a match for anyone at present charged with the management of troops of the line. Caesar was no more, nor Pompey . . . Despair set in with the knowledge of almost certain death as the only alternative. Death! According to our apocryphal historian Euxinus, Cleopatra had always been profoundly interested in the subject and surrounded herself with soothsayers and mages, taking the omens and distributing charms and propitiating the dark forces with gifts; she would hardly have been a Ptolemy and an Alexandrian otherwise.

But it was now, says Euxinus in his *The Secret Memorials*, that the omens turned clearly against them so that all counter-effort seemed vain.

"She hugged the idea of death to her like his body, imagining how it must be to pass through gravity's rainbow into the treasury of inorganic matter, present and future mingled and combined with the inhuman silence of all time, trodden like grapes in the presses of wishing."

Euxinus expands this text as follows:

"Antony had indeed surprised her, a simple unswerving soldier, not merely by his slouch-handsome address but by introducing a new idea to the asiatic queen: civic virtue as a useful instrument of government. At first the notion appeared to be so simple as to be almost comic. Virtue! She was tempted to give a little 'Pouf!' of amusement, so preposterous did it seem. But he said it with such a pleading look that she was touched. He was fine to the eye, like a young carnivore tasting meat after a long fast. He made other men seem tame and faceless when he uttered the word. 'Come,' she said with a smile, making room for him beside her on the bed, 'Come and sit beside me and tell me how to go about it. I love your name.'

"As a matter of fact there was more than a spark of sympathy, a likeness, between him and Agrippa, though his spirit seemed to her fine, whereas Agrippa the peasant was coarse-souled. At the back of her mind she was, however, ambitious and dreamed of conquering Rome with Antony at her side. In fact he was her tool as Agrippa was Octavian's. But Agrippa was not vain and his belief in the monarchy was part of his mystical patriotism; Antony was vain about his looks and proud of his spirit. Cleo was, after all, the last and most spirited of the Ptolemies; she could not dissociate herself from this god-given conjunction. The wild beauty and the fatigue which came from a long history of sleeplessness nibbled by drugs came further down the list, together with sudden tears about nothing. That is why the first premonition of utter disaster came over her when she realized that she had fallen in love with Antony, for that had not been on the original programme. Moreover it was precisely because of his worst, not best, qualities. It was a profane attachment which could only bring them sorrow, and made her feel lost and uneasy. Remember she was the granddaughter of Ptolemy the Devious and much preferred intrigue to bargaining — hence the role of courtesan she played in all her dealings with powerful men. She tried to think the whole matter through, of course, but she was poor at elaborating ideas. Her kiss now became the mere agent of stress and anguish. From Antony's point of view it was no less a disaster, for he realized that he had found his ignominious death through the ikon of a woman: one with no real substance. For she was a romantic wedded to notions of power and ambition.

"He lay there sleeping with his proffered erection: like a clock with only one hand. She unsheathed his sword and ran her fingers along the blade to test its keenness. She had nothing precise in mind about the suicide-act itself; she had gone completely vague inside, cloudy-vague — a mind without margins. Seeing her thus you might tell yourself that she realized now what death could be — cautious, meticulous and unsmiling, all things to all men. In the mirror she glimpsed a sardonic and prematurely aged nymph, slender as a beautiful yacht, doomed to snub out its life in sleep. She watched this beautiful purgatorial body with that great mane of chestnut hair which always refused ribbons and rostral crowns of olive. Actually she had planned the matter differently: they would die in each other's arms from the bite of a poisonous snake, but when it came to the touch the asp refused to perform, even though it began by hissing very satisfactorily. Her lover slept on, unaware of her confusion and vivid uncertainty, for deep inside she was superstitious about blood spilled — unless for religious reasons with due rites to mark the fact. This was a private expression of despair and not a civic or military necessity!

"It was humiliating to discover all this at the swordpoint. He was coarse, finally, a Roman pleb with the mind of a barber. He let out a snore at last and she woke him in disgust. It would have to be a sword, then? So be it!"

Grand Canal

Old men cry easily and wet their beds,
Incontinent in their dying as crowned heads
Death's keyhole they confront like newly weds.
Peach-fed survivors in their coffins of grace
They meet to mock their Maker face to face!

Resolve the chimera of free choice while we
Steadily become what we believe,
The discrete ego is our fatal fallacy
Hamlet dispensing his "to be or not to be"
And by the lantern of the finite mind
Set out to discover only what we find!
Nature's cruel version of Kant's double-bind.

If I must die in your welcome embrace
Bury me in this body half-asleep,
Woebegone, yes, but heartwhole, just to keep
The hounds of smiling passion in full cry.
Safe on the raft of your lovely body drift
Down through Mediterranean sigh by sigh
The spars of leaven-gold limbs spread wide
A pavilion of loving forms in postures meek
All night as Venice, monogram of the Holy Ghost, sails by.

The rot had set in, the slow spiral of disharmony and dis-integration had started to sap the foundations of the Roman ethos, the civic ethos which linked together, in firm religious union, civic sense, civic order, and the public happiness and social well-being which flowed from and shaped a comforting sense of wholeness. The idea of an individual and private religious field of understanding and operation was literally shocking to the Roman — perturbing even, for it bred sects which categorically refused to have anything to do with the formal worship of the people. "You refuse to go to our shows and processions," writes the outraged Minucius Felix in his *Octavius*, "You are never present at our public banquets, you shrink in disgust from our sacred games . . ." When Tacitus writes that the Christians were "the enemies of mankind," he was thinking of their explicit denial of everything which for the Roman spelt truth in practically a scientific sense. It was what made the world go round! For them there was no fact of human behaviour which was not distinguished by a profound piety. To share the behaviour of Jews and Chris-tians — it was unthinkably dangerous: it might stop the grass growing or the sun rising on the morrow. Quite apart from the fact that their behaviour was unctuous and self-righteous beyond belief, they believed themselves the chosen race, cho-sen by the monotheistic projection they worshipped, having duly warned all and sundry that this phantom was "a jealous god and would tolerate no other to compete with him." What a contrast to the tolerant, easy-going pluralism of Roman pantheism with its generous outlines, its gods and goddesses who were ever-present, in every communal activity, and as familiar to the devout public as film stars are today. They attested to the prime link with Mother Nature, not a with-drawal from it into a snobbish seclusion of sectarianism, each believer with his or her private and exclusive version of God. Moreover, the new theoretical concepts such as circumcision (ritual self-mutilation) were as disgusting as they were hap-

piness-destroying. "Atonement," "original sin," "guilt," "repentance" . . . One can glimpse the distraught, puzzled,
perhaps outraged expression of a Pilate or an Agrippa at this
kind of deliberate search for constraint, unhappiness, intellectual self-abuse before the immortal gods. For as the
pseudo-Cyprian writes elsewhere, "What is a theatrical performance without a god present, or a game without a sacrifice?"

Here was another bone of contention taken up by critics of
the Old Testament: "Jealous God," namely, "Sacrifice." But
if Rome was not built in a day, as the proverb runs, neither
was it destroyed in a night. The long and ignoble wrangle
about religious observance and the nature of the true god
had begun. It is an extraordinary story and is perhaps best
exemplified by the tale of Julian, the emperor known to history as "The Apostate," who after a long and agonizing period of incubation and secrecy felt at last called upon to reject
the Christian principle in its totality and opt for the ancient
faith which had served so well in the past: nothing less than
an open and avowed return to full paganism! The cat was
among the pigeons in no uncertain fashion. But Julian was
now sole emperor of his vast but splintered empire, and free
to act on his own fervent conviction. In a letter to his former
teacher Maximus he cannot stifle a note of jubilation at this
dramatic change of heart. "I worship the gods openly," he
says, "and the whole mass of the troops who are returning
with me worship the gods. I sacrifice oxen in public. I have
offered to the gods many hecatombs as thank-offerings. The
gods command me to restore their worship in its utmost
purity, and I obey them, yes, and with a good will." Indeed
on the subject of animal sacrifices to the gods he had almost
allowed it to become an obsession, so much did it delight
him after all the years of secrecy and dissimulation. When it
came to his plan to rebuild the Temple in an ambitious bid
for Jewish approval it was largely on the question of sacrifice

that he rested his claims to their attention. Although no longer practised, animal sacrifice had none the less once been an intrinsic and radical part of their religion. "Abraham used to sacrifice even as we Hellenes do, always and continually." Here he put his finger on a cardinal difference between the Jews and the Christians: sacrifice for the latter was unbloody, a ritual affair merely. But the animal sacrifice was quite current all over the Mediterranean. "Even to this day," writes the Emperor, "the Jews do sacrifice in their own houses . . . and give the right shoulder to the priests as the first-fruits." He seems to be thinking of ritual butchering. How persistent it is, the spilling of the dark blood with its theurgic appeal to the magician in man! The baroque bullfight is a lineal descendant of the ritual bloodspilling we know today as the Spanish *mise à mort* with all its flamboyant ritualistic magnificence. The proponents of the rite will be careful to point out that this is a combat and not just a cruel game, a gruesome relic of some ancient ritual whose magical significance still vibrates in the great Roman arenas of Provence. Sometimes at dawn you might come upon a lorry waiting to enter Arles with the dew, full of big black Iberian bulls soon to be decanted into the arenas as an offering to the rural gods of sport and combat. And the critics of the game will be brought up short with arguments at least as old as bloodshed itself. No, the black bull's death is not a wanton stroke, or fortuitous and without sense; it is as deliberate as it is purposeful. It evokes the earth-magic of full thunder, the tellurian electricity housed in the blood which flows into the red sand of the arenas, staining it like a draught of wine. It is transformed by the conjuror's passes of the black velvet cape from a simple air to a symphony which embodies a whole culture, falling in ruins, the dying bull. The blood staining the ground in a soundless sheet is the testament of the killer who kisses the sword with which he now dispatches the bull, softly passing the blade between the loosened vertebrae into the throbbing heart of the animal. The animal plunges deathward now into silence while 30,000 spectators set up a triumphant roar deeper than the sea. The ritual is complete.

The fissures of religious doubt and theological reservation ran from one end of the Empire to the other, creating vast holes through which the smoke of doubt drifted up, slowly, and formed critical fields of action, just what the Roman ethos wished to avoid: doubt, confusion, scepticism which leads in the end to aberrant behaviour, revolution in fact. One could see now just how tactfully and kindly the ancient ethos which ruled pagan thought had operated in the field of ordinary day-to-day civic behaviour. From our modern point of view the ancients who lived in this fashion were far more "religious" than the doleful bigots who were now struggling to replace them. For the Roman there was no act one could commit which did not fall within the orbit of some god's influence. In other words, one could do nothing which was not shadowed by a deity. Man lived his life completely permeated by the influences of nature, and his gods and goddesses were like kindly uncles and aunts, part of a vast but not intimidating family. Now this entire coherent set of beliefs and attitudes was at risk from Christians and Jews — meddlesome fanatics with a thirst for power as symbolized by gold, plus an unerring taste for the meretricious wherever it was fund-raising: the *moulin à sous* of the Jewish mind displacing the Christian prayer-wheel which the advocates of Jesus promoted. The end of the wrangle was the crucifixion of Jesus: the *mise à mort* of insight, to placate the wrath of a guilt-engendering god. These sectarian squabbles were not just superficial: they cut deep, modifying conduct, says Celsus, the ablest of the critics of the time.

Celsus was firmly against the new sectarian tendencies being evolved through Christianity, because they represented the transfer of religious values from the public sphere to that of a private association. These self-righteous separatists not only refused military service but also declined to accept public office, or to assume any responsibility in the government of cities. It was, however, not simply that Christians subverted the cities by refusing all participation in civic life; they undermined the societies in which they were actually living. By setting up their Founder as someone of divine status they posed a rival to the one high God who watched over the whole Empire and its interlacing scheme of pagan entities.

"But," continues Celsus, "there is nothing wrong if each people observes its own laws of worship. In fact we find the differences between nations very considerable yet each finds its own system the best. The Ethiopians who live at Meroe worship only Zeus and Dionysus, the Arabians Ourania and Dionysus. The Egyptians worship Isis and Osiris . . . Then some abstain from sheep, reverencing them as sacred, others from goats, others from crocodiles . . ."

Rome's lenient and tactful form of government had managed to tether together all these dissimilar forces of belief and action into a way of life which offered peace and security to the ordinary citizen. Now the whole of this age-old fabric was at risk.

The sweet fable of Roman peace was being repudiated by Christian and Jew alike. The world broke up into sectarian splinter-movements, a hundred mutually incompatible beliefs and usages. And secret societies whose clandestine acts and meetings troubled the governors of cities. Often the Christians were accused of undercover beliefs, of secret banquets including feasts of human flesh thrust upon initiates of the new religion. These recall the so-called Thyestean banquets named after Thyestes, who seduced his brother's wife and was then invited to dinner at which his sons were served up to him. Ritual meals of human flesh, orgies involving promiscuous intercourse, and sacrificial murder are also described in the Greek novel of Lollanios, known as the Cologne Papyrus. The Histories of Livy, which were written in the reign of Augustus, have much to tell us of the Bacchic orgies of these groups, the indiscriminate coupling of the members and the ecstatic wild dancing bouts in the forests. In the interests of civic order these bacchanalia were banned from Rome itself and placed under a somewhat half-hearted police control. But sometimes the Christians and Jews got branded as secret postulants in these extravagant doings.

What was beginning to drift up through the fissures and rents in the ancient polytheistic systems were fragments of archaic beliefs, chunks of animism left over from the detritus of the old version of civic habit centred in primitive doctrine. Theurgy is the word which best sums it up, standing for the belief that the divine can be approached through "magical" acts, such as the use of salves and ointments, herbs and roots, garlic and hellebore. Iamblichus the philosopher was quite explicit that "it was not thinking which linked men with the divinity but the efficacy of the unspeakable acts performed in the appropriate manner, acts beyond comprehension and powerful because of the potency of the unutterable symbols which are clear only to the divinity . . ." One way of effecting union with the divinity was by animating statues in order to extract oracles from them. By the use of incense, herbs, scents and special chants and prayers, the devotee sought to induce a statue to smile or nod or in some other way respond to one's entreaty with a sign. And each god had his sympathetic representation in the animal, vegetable or mineral world. One was adventuring into the world of archetypal symbols and forms where secrecy is the law, not for any other reason than that the transcendental vision or experience simply outstrips the resources of language to do justice to it, far less to describe it. In this domain of true alchemy poetry is the only resource!

All this matter is highly relevant to the country loosely called Provence, owing to the continuity of its historic patterns. A simple example: the new flock of high-speed trains — expresses labelled TGV — all carry the heraldic insignia of their native county. Those which serve the Gard all bear the escutcheon (palm tree, chain, crocodile, cloud) which Octavian ordered the mint to strike for the memorial coin to the Actium victory. For someone who has lived very much in the shadow of the Pont du Gard and Agrippa, it is touching to see these giant locomotives, so like hideous beetles, come whirling into Nîmes with their heraldic shields proudly sported. Yet in many years of residence I have found very few people who knew the provenance of these insignia and even today I am always being asked what they mean. Poor Cleopatra! On the platform at Nîmes, by the same token of historic continuity you might find some dark soothsayers from Gabon or Senegal selling *gris-gris*, lucky charms against impotence. Examine them and you will find they are little wax emblems of the sex organs, male or female, linked in a sweet theurgic invocation to the gods of fertility. Yoni and Lingam!

Béziers: roses, rivers, rain and ruins

So death ad hoc
Or love ad lib
And memory da capo
To get back what you give.
With the taxonomy of lust,
Doctors so keen on being right.
"I think therefore I must
Before the poor survivors turn to dust!"

But once the circle of initiation closes
A death-begotten insight rules,
Rough harness of the old anxieties,
Offer their trivial psychoses,
Models for human fools.

Lawrence Durrell

But most of us after the fatal
Déclic, thrust of the love-mind,
Will go on living paranormally
A post-humous life so to speak to find
In some cold garage of a human love,
Full of defenceless corpses smiling up,
Already embalmed and sailing away
So blessed are the meek, so limitlessly weak,
The ruins of the moon pressed cheek to cheek
"I love, wherefore should I seek?"
Smiling through children's tears they seem to say.

The truth is that Provence is a very strange place, and not entirely reassuring, particularly the mountainous parts with their mining towns and withdrawn Protestant communities who live out a life of secret repudiation. I think even the modern tourist feels the deep introspective undertow of a certain melancholy, which prompts one to ask an unusual question which sounds more mediaeval than Roman, namely, "Is there not something profoundly morbid at the heart of all beauty?" Despite the rich colour and magnificent display of the earth's riches which make the place so obviously the prototype for the Garden of Eden, it had to be lived in with caution and prescience by its true inhabitants, the Provençaux, who were securely anchored in their language and their national poetry with its wild romanticism and warmth of style. The truth is that they are only French by proxy, by accident, and the land is only demographically so. Provence is about as French as Wales is English — in other words, not at all! The demographic myth is a convenience accepted with a cheerful unwillingness: the post office decrees it! But once you have a whole language of your own and a poet or two like Mistral to sanctify it, you have a real country of your own which is like no other on earth. People who at a deep level know what it is to be Scottish, Irish or Welsh will recognize at once what the word Provençal means from this point of view. That the land should play the role of summer playground for the whole wide world changes nothing, for it is an excellent shop window for its wines and other produce, and its charming fairs simply brim with the products of its husbandry. But still the key word for the Provençal soul remains *félibre*, by which Mistral proposed to designate the poets of Provence, true descendants of the troubadours who found their spiritual sources in the Courts of Love which presided over the emergent European spirit in Les Baux.

But Provence is also geographically an open-ended country and subject to fluctuations of population, not only the tourist invasion of summer with its three months of colourful celebrations, but also the vast number of illegal residents about whom the police try in vain to keep records. A recent official count suggested that there were some 40,000 persons who had entered the country and then just melted away, leaving no trace of their existence! And once the summer fêtes of the coast begin their infernal cycle of music and paint and sport, the whole of Paris crowds in, bringing its criminals with it. Africa is also present in force: Senegal, Gabon, from far away or near at hand: Sfax, Alexandria, Algiers . . .

The continuous intellectual ferment which set in and heralded the end of the Roman Empire's stability became particularly evident from about the second century, and is traceable today in the writings which have come down to us. The documentation is dense and various and it shows that the whole of religious and philosophic belief had come under intense scrutiny, with a widespread scepticism about the validity of the old world's convictions and attitudes. The propositions concerning nature and man evolved by Plato and Aristotle were increasingly set at risk by the intellectual aberrations of new sects and societies which were active contenders for popular belief.

Whether you take the writing of a major thinker of scientific genius like Galen, or the simpler historic talent of an ex-governor like Pliny, you cannot escape the conviction that a steady drift into scepticism and doubt had set in, and the new faith, Christianity, was only one of several beliefs seeking to allay it. Even a superficial examination of Galen's writing shows us that to the thinkers of his time Christian and Jewish thought was profoundly at odds with the classical Greek conception of the relation of man to God, and God to the world. Galen makes no bones about it. These new intransigents were seen as profoundly objectionable for they were dogmatic and quite uncritical, and unwilling to submit their beliefs to philosophic examination. The implicit monotheism they propounded was also profoundly distasteful to the Roman mind, which had been forged by a classical poetry and a polytheistic latitude towards nature and man . . . Nevertheless, if the new beliefs took time to acclimatize themselves, the new atmosphere of qualified beliefs or downright doubts went far towards sapping the foundations of civil life, for to the Roman mind civic order and belief were by origin religious predispositions.

This was recently brought home to me very forcibly at the site of Romana Narbona, present-day Narbonne, all that is left of a once great capital which had been raised in the shelter of a lagoon and did an extensive Mediterranean trade. As a Roman colony of the first rank, founded at the same time as Arles, it had naturally enjoyed a forum, capitol, baths, spacious amphitheatre, theatre and many temples to appropriate deities. Alas, little remains today save the silhouette, the merest shadow of its age of greatness. For in the modern town one is nagged by a feeling of incompleteness, almost of inconsequence; nevertheless, despite the playful architectural amendments of Viollet-le-Duc, Narbonne cathedral is a delight to the eye after a prolonged diet of castellated fortress-churches of early date. It is of the fourteenth century, light, aerial and lantern-like, with glorious flying buttresses winging their way straight to God! But the church, which is unfinished, still has no nave, only the lovely soaring choir standing out like a stone entreaty. What has gone wrong? Is it perhaps a matter of scale, one cannot help asking oneself? The archiepiscopal palace was in the first intention a fortress with two stout towers. Viollet-le-Duc, fresh from his triumphant if theatrical amendments to Avignon, was invited by the town to take the building in hand and to produce a façade to join the towers in a suitable fashion; it was thence to be the façade of the Hôtel de Ville. Emboldened by his success with the walls of Avignon, where the buttresses run up unstaged and are then united by eloquent arches of uncompromising boldness to sustain parapet and battlements, he resolved to try the same thing with the Narbonne project. But he inadvertently reduced the scale of the new piers and the whole project seems to have withered in the execution. It lacks the theatrical flamboyance which is his hallmark and the only excuse for his somewhat jovial approach to these hallowed shrines. One wonders whether Agrippa would have shared the rather unresponsive modern judgement on such bold, incautious work. On the other hand, everything has its time of ripeness and personally I would not be without Viollet-le-Duc's world despite the coarseness of vision, of sensibility it suggests. It is perfectly congruent with a world of cut-rate tourism and cinema. (I believe that in America a cinema company managed to find a market for old sets of famous films or fragments thereof; the public is still willing to pay to traipse around them, still mesmerized by the glamour of the silver screen.)

But Narbonne, like Avignon and Nîmes, is rich in Roman relics which managed to escape the wholesale pillage of the Middle Ages — the walls of all these amazing fortresses were raised with the stones burgled from the Roman remains. Time passes, and history moves apace, while the ensuing jerk of the time-field creates a new shift of sensibility, a new consciousness which records itself in a changed habit. In this context I could make a reference to the prevalence of late Roman towns which have freedmen's caps sculpted on them. They give a pleasant touch of oddity to the stone plaque but they also provide the historian with a clue to a sudden shift of insight in patrician Rome.

When a noble Roman died (I am not sure when the cult started) his will declared that a certain number of his slaves were to be freed in order for him to reap the rewards of his virtuous act in the Afterworld. Moreover, this act was to be recorded by the sculpture on his funerary stone of freedmen's caps, so many slaves per cap, as it were. In this way the whole world could take stock of a virtuous end and offer up suitable admiration. And the cap itself has come down to history as a symbol of liberty: either the peaked ones as featured in the stories of Robin Hood and his outlaws, or the Basque beret type of cap such as one sees at the Wailing Wall in Jerusalem adopted by certain Jewish sects to express the same sentiments. But what is so striking about these sculpted Roman caps is that they indicate something which we did not believe formed part of the Roman consciousness: namely, any idea of freedom whatsoever, or any real admission that Rome, for all its virtues and splendours, was founded completely upon slave labour. And finally, that there was anything desirable about the state of freedom . . . Our historians have yet to tell us how this came about: dare we suspect Christianity or Mithraism? The value of the individual soul echoed the value of the individual person, from exactly when I cannot say. Perhaps this new consciousness grew up some time after Actium. It was a period of change, of intense self-questioning. It was obvious that the new Principate needed a large standing army to police the borders of its far-flung Empire, and in 13 BC a new-style army was declared, open as a career to all citizens with a nominal duration of twenty years, steady pay and a lump sum on retirement. (Of course these sums were quite

often dwarfed by imperial gifts after successful campaigns —
hence the founding of Nîmes, Arles, Béziers, etc.). And of
course as time went on the Emperor's own titles depended
more and more on the firm loyalty of the army and its moods.
By modern standards it does not seem numerically outra-
geous either: the twenty-eight or so legions comprised about
16,000 men supported by an equal number of professional
provincial auxiliaries, while Rome itself boasted of the famous
praetorian guard, urban cohorts, *vigiles*. In addition there was
a tactical fleet army divided up into several groups and located
at Ravenna, Misenum and elsewhere.

Some momentous change in the spiritual climate was at
hand, and the gradual extinction of Rome as a world power
can be effectively studied if we take one single capital city
which lived through the dramatic changes. I am thinking of
Arles or Nîmes. In a model summary of the Roman history
of these later years, T. A. Cook wrote:

"There is no doubt that for a long time after the full confir-
mation of Augustus in his power the vices of his successors
fell upon the capital alone, and it was the blessings of their
ordered rule that were enjoyed by Provence. Even the bloodshed and disorder that followed the death of Marcus Aurelius
did not prevent the prosperity of Arles continuing for another
sixty years. But it is significant that the magnificent gladiatorial shows provided in her amphitheatre by the Emperor
Gallus in October of AD 254 were given to celebrate a successful treaty of peace with the Goths, whose leader, Crocus,
eventually pillaged the city and destroyed many of its monuments only six years afterwards. It was entirely due to the
favour of Constantine that she ever recovered. The greatness
of her Roman existence rose, indeed, to its highest point
under the reign of that enlightened Emperor, whose palace
is still represented on the banks of the Rhone by the ruined
tower called La Trouille. . . . By the munificence of Constan-

tine the public and the imperial buildings of Arles rose to a greater splendour than had ever been seen before; and with him the Christian religion had become the religion of the throne. . . . Already the first great Council of the Church had been summoned by Constantine and attended by the bishops of York, Trèves, Milan, and Carthage and many more, under the primacy of the Bishop of Arles."

The patchwork quilt of provinces had begun slowly to mobilize itself into a coherent administrative identity; for example the city was picked out by Honorius in AD 418 as the meeting place of the seven provinces of Gaul. There too in AD 455 Avitus was proclaimed Emperor in the Alyscamps while Theodoric and his Goths looked on . . . The last flicker of Roman pre-eminence comes when the Court of Majorian is set up in AD 458, in the very palace of the great Constantine himself. It is almost the end of things, for the eight-month siege of the town follows. Arles fell to the Visigoths in the spring of AD 468, and henceforth the rule of Rome was extinguished for good and all. All that remains is the present harvest of marvellous inscribed stones which still crowd the museums of the land and which can still teach us a great deal about the new shift of consciousness which followed on the arrival of Christianity . . .

"It is fashionable to deplore the last victories of Christianity with its gradual tilting back into paranoia and frustration, but it is difficult to see how things could have fallen out differently," says Aldo in the commonplace book. "Something has gone wrong with the blood-count of the rulers. They have dwindled into colourless flavourless sub-personalities, inconsequential rulers, bloodthirsty freaks. We should not waste time or pity on them. But as philosophers we have a right to deplore the predisposition towards monotheism that set in and coaxed our thinkers through pragmatism to a final scientific determinism which is responsible for many of our ills."

But from the harvest of stones which have been gathered and catalogued in Arles alone, we can trace very clearly the shift of mood and tense in post-Roman thinking. The most striking difference, both in treatment and subject-matter, is to be found in the early Christian monuments which form the most riveting part of the unparalleled collection of Roman sarcophagi held by the city today, and which are on view to the public. A brief visit cannot help but render a modern visitor thoughtful. *The pagans approached death so cheerfully.* Their monuments exhale a smiling, guileless happiness almost worthy of Chinese sages.

The so-called pagans carved upon a dead man's tomb only an agreeable recollection of the happiest scenes of everyday life: the vine-gatherings, the olive-plantings, the picnics, the hunting excursions, the story-tellings or recitations. Or they gave a frank and free expression to the best art they considered appropriate to his memory. For them the dead could still be cherished thus in memory. But once Christianity sets in, all the slender grace of these plastic conceptions vanishes, to be replaced by subject matter which is as rueful as it is lugubrious: hairy saints and bowed mourners, sanctimonious goblins from a world of guilt and repentance whose very salvation hovers over them as a sort of threat: castration, fear, repression. The early tombs reveal the new trend with a ghastly clarity. The expression in these figures reveals an intensity of conviction which makes you forget their enormous hands, unwieldy heads and pitiful, disproportionate limbs and bodies.

One thing stands out with startling clarity — another shift of key, but a big one. Where the Roman took his happiness and fulfilment from the past, the early Christian looked forward fervently to a nebulous notion of a *future* which was an integral factor of a passionately trusted creed. His fulfilment was future-oriented! One realizes too from such a comparison the value of the Roman system which was now disintegrating.

After all, from the five whole centuries of Roman imperial rule in Gaul we have records in medals, inscriptions, monuments and tombs, besides actual written records. Nowhere do we find hatred of the Empire as such among these remains. Emperors might be personally criticized in Gaul, just as they were by Tacitus and Juvenal in Rome: but the imperial system was as highly honoured there as here. Even when Gaul had the choice of her own destiny in the third century, completely apart from Italian influence, she chose an Emperor. Nor were the inhabitants ever disarmed. The paltry thirty legions of the Empire could never have controlled so many millions except by consent, had not their political ideals gradually become identical . . . The monarchy was universally beloved. It fulfilled a profound need. After all, near Lyon, at the confluence of those two great rivers Rhône and Saône, sixty tribal federations joined together to consecrate a common shrine to Rome and Augustus, the rites being served by prominent Gauls who had held office in their own country and who were publicly thanked for their devotion to the rich common altar. Roman political history is a tangled skein indeed when one thinks of the great varieties of tribes and races which went to make up the whole. The craft of holding the whole organism together was much more than could be attributed to a disciplined army. The whole thing was calibrated by a superlative political sense, a highly evolved sense of crowd psychology. In this domain the name that swims up out of the ground is always that of Caesar. It is his name that echoes on among the tumbled stones and pillaged monuments of this smiling countryside, and one can do nothing as pleasant as to follow his history — his Provençal history — picnic by picnic as it were, and township by township: St-Rémy, Carpentras, Orange, Marseille. But to do this it is best to set up — as he himself would have done — a camp, a headquarters for such an operation. For this purpose I would propose St-Rémy.

Provence

I know of few villages more benign, and indeed more beautiful for a prolonged visit, say in April; its green and radiant glades give off a feeling of a perennial rejuvenating and healing force. The feeling, the light, conveys a magical playfulness, almost boisterousness; it is as if here the inhabitants wake up in a good humour every morning. It is like a corner of Greece. I ran across a letter written before the war concerning such a visit made at that epoch, travelling by the jumping and skipping little railway from Tarascon, irresponsible as a spring lamb it seemed. You crossed the broad and smiling valleys which led to this pearl among hamlets where the battered old Hôtel de Provence was waiting, its owner sitting outside his own front door on a fallen slab of Roman masonry reading the local gazette's account of the latest bullfight at nearby Sommières — a cockade-snatching, to be sure. Beside him on a rough table under a tree he will already have set out a bottle and glasses because, as he is never tired of affirming, "Une visite s'arrose" (a visitation should be toasted). No true Provençal would ever contest such a sentiment. As for myself, though not conspicuously pious, I readily fell in with it. At that period, too, most of the village girls wore the magnificent costume of the land, so that they looked like the smiling nymphs of Tanagra in human, fleshly statuette — as if they had stepped off the dusty shelves of the museums and straight into everyday life. The streets of the village were avenues of plane trees garlanded with creepers in full flower, little hanging balls of flower worked by the wasps and bees with classical industry. The sleepy music of their call filled the air, which was pervaded with the dense scents of syringa, of roses and of shady limes. Apart from the silver groves of piously pruned and tended olives protected by the buttresses of the Alpilles, the gardens are the chief business of the little town. Seeds are still grown for all the horticulturalists of France — and for many in England also.

But the real *genius loci*, the animating spirit which informs everything here, dwells in the neighbouring village of Maillane, home of Mistral, the poet who has added form and identity to the language and spirit of the real inner Provence, now being consistently sapped by the attitude of tourist offices and the information they disburse so prolifically. At the time of which I write there was very little road traffic. It was well before the era of autoroutes. Mostly, the temptation was to walk to places like Maillane carrying a rucksack on one's back for the journey. I am lucky to have seen Provence in this way, before the massacre of the planes.

But the memories which cluster about St-Rémy will also be forever inextricably bound up with the resonance of those sumptuous potations and no less sumptuous conversations ushered in by my friends, the poets and painters of the château who dropped in on Aldo unheralded, each with his private obsession to be indulged or a work-in-progress to be nursed along. In St-Rémy the anchor of our sentimental attachment was inevitably Caesar-oriented because of the splendid lyrical pyramidal monument on the Plateau des Antiquités which for long was classified as a Mausoleum. It was inevitable, too, that these rambling historical arguments forced us to look anew into Plutarch to get some sort of evaluation of the character of these giants of the past. Naturally our speculations did not always err on the side of orthodoxy, for we felt free to call in the odd observation of Euxinus to fill in a landscape wanting in details. "After all," as Aldo pointed out, "it is the anomalies of history which give one the fun, for history so often jumps the points. One pace to right or left and you get a change of epicentre which changes the whole field of observation. It can take centuries or it can happen in a flash. Sometimes this momentous gleam of the new consciousness has an immediate effect, sometimes nothing is sparked off."

Myself, I often think of the afternoon when suddenly the

Provence

Arabs introduced the notion and the sign for "zero" into the existing mathematics of the time. Suddenly one wonders what the Romans had done up till then with their idea of nothingness: was it a thing, a tangible element; or just a hole in space, just as for the Greeks the word *Eu-topia* mean literally *Not-a-place*? At any rate it was a radical shift of key in Roman thinking to replace the great clumsy Roman numerals with these economical aerial ciphers, specially the one from India called "zero!" (Zero was inert, could not be used as a divisor. A new abstract version of negation — loneliness looking for a mate, you might say.) Was it the first sneaking intimation of a tentative version of what later reared its head as The Principle of Indeterminacy? When the Cyclops, peering into the shadows, cried, "Who goes there?" and Ulysses replied "Nobody," he was making the first philosophic joke about the nature of reality — poetic reality. But I see Aldo shake his head and say, "Too alembicated by half!" He is right to distrust ideas which have been over-elaborated. And yet . . . Mathematical reality has its poetic side.

The thrilling elegance of the erection in praise of Marius, and the triumphal arch — though rudely battered by time and the subsequent wars — dominate the feelings of aesthetic richness which one enjoys in contemplating them. The evening light is best. On the green sward of the nearby fields one will almost certainly hear the evocative ticking of bowls, as certain an accompaniment to the drowsy Provençal evening as the tick-tock of cricket balls marks the corresponding afternoon languors of an English village — or did in time past. It is worth noting that the chief items of aesthetic pleasure, the Maison Carrée of Nîmes, and the two stone obelisks of St-Rémy, all give one the feeling of light, aerial execution which makes one think of them as being predominantly Greek in influence, for whatever the distinction is worth. We must not forget to what an extent the ethos of Greece formed the moral foundation for whatever came after it in the form of Rome;

physically, too, Greek craftsmen, Greek artists have moved westward into the Roman field and taken their skills with them. They confided to their workmanship a beauty like a sort of spiritual nimbleness expressed in the stone they expanded upon the taut blueness of the Provençal sky. Beside their work the Roman touch was a trifle cumbersome, at its worst even podgy. The Greek artefact expressed a patrician tact and a flawless good taste.

"The base of the St-Rémy monument measures about twenty-two feet each way: the total height is over sixty feet; and it needs no great effort of the imagination to see in this exquisite piece of proportion the model of many early mediaeval church steeples in this part of Provence." Thus Cook, who waxes somewhat lyrical about St-Rémy, as well he might. And he continues: "Few other leaders could have dared posterity to make comparison between their own campaigns and that which annihilated the invading Northerners beneath the crags of Mont Ste-Victoire. But Julius Caesar was able, without fear of comment, to erect the arch to his own triumph over Vercingetorix beside the monument of the general which he set up at St-Rémy, as he had restored the monuments of the great popular leader in the streets of Rome.

There is a political as well as a military significance in these buildings . . . Marius had returned to Rome after his Provençal victories as the leader of the popular party. His military reforms had at once democratized the army, and attached it more closely to its leader . . . He was the champion of the Italian middle class, and by them he was made consul, especially to combat socialistic schemes on one side, and aristocratic exclusiveness and luxury on the other. Unfortunately he arrived too late. The future was with the nobly born, the aristocratic Caesar, and Caesar saw at once that it was by posing as the people's champion, as the nephew of Marius and the son in law of Cinna, that he would finally succeed!"

The qualities which were now coming to the fore were as radical as his military judgement; they were those of an incomparable political tactician. To these I think we have a right to add the quality of sheer charm, a force of character so seductive that it almost amounted to crowd-hypnotism. He was able to exact from the primitive tribes surrounding Provence a devotion and fidelity which even at this late remove seems disproportionate to the simple facts of the case — like his logistic strengths, for example. Cook once again:

"To the south of St-Rémy these marvellous buildings stand on the north side of the scarred and sun-scorched crags of the Alpilles, true Provençal hills: barren yet beautiful: grey, lilac, gold against the setting sun, but never green . . . From the lower part of the great camp where Marius awaited the Barbarians they look out over the plain that extends as far as Avignon, that is bounded by the horizon of Mont Ventoux and of the hills that guard Vaucluse. Behind them, to the south, begin the crags crowned by the dusty solitudes of the fortress of Les Baux, by the misery and squalor of these mediaeval ruins that are in such terrible contrast to the sane and beautiful relics of classical antiquity."

One of the sadnesses of Provence is the sense that with the emergence of the Jealous God with his sclerotic uniformity of countenance the real decline began, and it has steadily continued until today when, as Aldo gloomily says, "You can read your Spengler aloud over an open grave!" It seems clear to us now that the real predator and despoiler of nature is man, and that whenever and wherever he appears, the well-being of simple humanity is seriously at risk: the triumph of cupidity, negligence and selfishness rules! Moreover this time it seems highly probable that the rate of the destruction of our natural resources has outrun the capacity for natural repair.

As for the flower-filled St-Rémy of today, the little village has kept all its charms. After Marius had passed on, some Romans and some Greeks were left, and among them were absorbed the ancient Celtic populations in the new town of Glanum which only became St-Rémy in the eleventh century. But the site has produced pottery of every kind. Poke at any of the mud walls of this pottery-land and smashed fragments will rain down; the black and fragile paste of Celtic ware, the delicate gold and honey-coloured pottery of the Greeks which is light enough to float on water (for night lights!), then also the friable pottery of the Arabs, varnished to hold liquids safely and ornamented with lines and geometrical patterns, and the thick red sturdy ware of solid Roman provenance. They will be very much to the forefront of your thoughts as, rucksack on your back, you march down the quiet dusty roads towards the only living Provençal shrine, the house of her national poet. Roads flooded with spring sunshine and verdant with the strange green palpitating shadows thrown by those lofty pinnacles of cypress that rise dark, sheer, yet delicate as cathedral walls: protection from the tremendous onslaughts of that demonic wind, the mistral. If your journey falls upon a day of wind it will prove a really memorable experience, for the whole landscape seems to be under full sail, its trees and shrubs in full contortion, trying to take off and ascend into the dazed blue sky. Provence! Mistral! The words are almost synonymous — or should be . . .

Visiting Orange

All airs and graces, their prevailing wind
Blows through the tapestry to stiffen
The fading girls, complexions of tea-roses,
With pets upon provincial laps
And hair combed back against the grain

Provence

In innocent professional poses
Sit centred, watching time elapse.

Scented abundance of black hair built back
In studied rolls of merchandise to loom
Over strangers' visitations: ladies of pleasure.
Their musical instruments are laid aside,
Oh! lethargy of educated leisure
That palls and yawns between these silken walls.
But one, luckier or younger, stands apart
On a far bridge to enjoy a private wish,
Casting the aquiline fishing-rod of gold
Angling for other kinds of fish.

– IX –

Woman in Provence

In a country so full of variety in its monuments and so full
of marvels of every epoch, it seems almost invidious to single
out some for special praise at the expense of the rest; but one
is forced to do so in the interests of order and coherence.
Among the most arresting by its strangeness is undoubtedly
the weird limestone fastness which is called Les Baux, and
which offers the traveller the chance of a picnic he will not
soon forget. This little town, set high on its white limestone
perch, can be included in a circular itinerary which could take
one from Arles to St-Rémy as well, with a return journey to
Arles via Tarascon. Thus the extensive Roman remains at
Glanum with their historic echoes could be consulted by the
historian, and the noble sweep of the tree-lined Rhône admired in Tarascon. But Les Baux . . .

About 12 miles from St-Gabriel the rather melancholy chain
of hills shoots out a southerly arm which suddenly veers up
from the plain and forms a plateau at the summit, encrusted
with white crags and scrub. This plateau is not completely
flat, but slightly tilted to the westward and here there looms
the enigmatic deserted township called Les Baux, surely one
of the most romantic and picturesque sites in the whole country, even though its present emptiness invests it with a

tremendous and indeed sinister atmosphere. The whole town seems to have been carved and shaped in lump sugar: the friable whitish stone easily answers to the mason's chisel. It is in fact bauxite by origin and was so named after the site where its existence was first put on record. But the nagging feeling of gloom, almost despair, generated by the whole place is mostly due to the isolation and the total emptiness of what must once have been a magnificent baroque township topped by a castle with glorious views from the high donjon. But . . . eagles turn slowly in the sky, and the wind echoes shrilly in the hollows of the keep. The stone-carved tombs of vanished Saracens are full of weeds and tall grasses, where the only moving things are the lizards avid for sunlight. And here the whole stage-set lies, the natural cliffs sculpted and perforated to form whole mansions — window and door, vault and hall, balcony and keep. The climb is a stiff one, and also the ascent by a well-defended castle keep and donjon. The ribbon of street reminds one at once of Petra and also Pompeii, and the whole breathlessly empty of human life. A far-away tinkle of a bell hints at the presence of a flock of sheep or goats somewhere out of sight on the mountain.

That is all.

But, like most of the historic sites in this part of Provence, Les Baux seems almost over-endowed with historic echoes, and the longest period of unchanged government seems to have been initiated in 1642 when Louis XIII declared it a marquisate and ceded it to the house of Monaco ruled by Prince Honoré Grimaldi; it stayed as part of the Monaco inheritance right up to the Revolution of 1789.

Long before this settling of the dust of history, the barony of Les Baux consisted of a confusing jumble of castle and properties which was grouped together (79 *bourgs* or towns) for geographical convenience under the collective title of La Baussenique. This rich and various landship was coveted by Louis III, Duke of Anjou and Count of Provence, and confiscated in 1414, after having been governed by one family from Pons des Baux who died in 970, though the last male representative did not disappear until 1374. The tomb of Raymond des Baux, who was the Grand Chamberlain to Queen Jeanne of Naples, bears the inscription, "To the illustrious family of the Baux, which is held to derive its origin from the ancient kings of Armenia, to whom, under the guidance of a star, the Saviour of the World manifested Himself."

Indeed, the ruined chapel of St-Claude still carries in the bosses of the vaulting the arms of these long-dead princes and other noble families who lived here in this empty township and were their feudatories. The arms of Baux represented a star, for they claimed direct descent from Balthazar, one of the Magi who came from the East bringing gifts for the Infant Saviour. It is difficult, in listening to a recital of their titles, not to feel the melancholy weight of mediaeval history — podestas of Milan, consul-podestas of Arles where they had a castle, seneschals of Piedmont, justiciaries of the kingdom of Naples, princes of Orange, viscounts of Marseille . . .

And that is not the whole catalogue, for they could also claim the title of Counts of Provence, Kings of Arles and Vienne, princes of Achaia, counts of Cephalonia, and they ended by being able to claim to be Emperors of Constantinople! What a cocktail party! Walking the length of this honeycomb of a place, which seems to have been ripped up and overturned by some giant's hands, you can reflect appropriately on the caprices of history and the cruelties of pomp and circumstance. Nothing will answer you back except the wind among the stones brushing the occasional cluster of wild violets.

As I write these lines I think of the recent death of that smiling philosopher of love, Denis de Rougemont; perhaps there is a sad appropriateness about the fact, for there is no modern writer who so thoroughly felt and expressed

Provence as he did in his *L'Amour et l'Occident** which, after its initial international success, has settled down most deservedly as a great twentieth-century classic. Indeed it is he who should have embarked upon this chapter of the hypothetical book instead of me. And not merely because his documentation was flawless. It is because the role played by woman was capital in forging the European sensibility, and with it the literature that was to follow this dark age, stretching from the eleventh to the fifteenth century with its gradually overwhelming presence of the cathedrals, like floating liners echoing with the trump of organ music and choirs: Paris, Chartres, Laon, Amiens, Reims . . . But it was here in Provence, not anywhere else, that romantic love was invented or at any rate received its courtly sanction as a form of metaphysical inquiry. The poetry was the outer skin of the quest. And as the great pagan civilization of Rome went down in slow ruin like a prize bull, the remnants of the Roman metaphysic — the gods and nymphs who up till then controlled the natural world with their old haunting presences — began to reflect a Europe plunging down into full dispersion, broken up by the contesting claims of different creeds and races. But underneath all this ferment woman was busy forging a place for herself in the scheme of things, as well as outlining a model upon which the European sensibility could base itself. Thus came about that unexpected and indeed bizarre convention — or was it just a parlour game? — known as the Courts of Love, which the modern scholar is still a little wary of accepting; indeed some modern scholarship has tried to throw doubt upon the existence of such courts, but we have enough evidence to the contrary, and can afford to accept their singularity wholeheartedly.

Their smiling code was far from being a mockery of civil justice, though the pattern was the same. The proceedings

---

*Translated as *Love in the Western World*.

took place under the patronage of some great beauty, a châtelaine of renown, and these meetings brought together not only the flower of the gentry but the most refined wits, minstrels, court poets. The living convention seems to have been invented in the Midi and to have slowly travelled north from castle to castle, from beauty to beauty. Many factors came together to ensure the success of the convention. It provided winter company for the bold bad barons of the day, especially prized during the closed season, for Provence has winters which, though short, are quite brutal; and one cannot spend one's whole life in the hunting field. Furthermore, the Courts of Love with their meticulous code and fine observance provided a sort of exercise and education for the rude sensibilities of these steel-clad men who gloried in the name "*Fervestus*," meaning "the iron-clad one" — the mediaeval version of "macho!"

All this was something more than a smiling social conceit, a plea for fair play for the fair sex, for sportsmanship in love . . . Great beauties of the day, sure of themselves, could play at a quasi-jurisdiction over lovers' hearts and their consequent behaviour. Whole sensibilities were evoked in this poetry and educated in fine sentiment. The love poetry tried to fathom the nature of Eros, to realize him through the code. This is what makes institutions like the Courts of Love at Les Baux so original and so poignant, the struggle of the courtly poets (the troubadours) so instructive; it was so much more than an upper-class frivolity, a bagatelle of the sentimental or high-minded ladies of Provence. It was an attempt to provide a school with a code not just of morals but of aesthetics as well. The subject, of course, was love — love in its poetic dimension! Here we come upon a charming paradox. It is the strong influence of Spanish Muslim ideas upon the love-code. The Persian love-poets like Djalal al-Din Rumi played a distinct part in formulating the more esoteric part of the code: the mixture of sexual ecstasy and transcendent evocation, the dark side of the moon, derived strong impulses from such sources. It is strange to reflect that had it not been for Charles Martel the whole of Europe would have been Muslim today!

We can see how through such apparent games the great lady of the day was busy trying to insist on a style, a code, within which love, that rarest of sentiments, could find its own values. She was pleading for a new sportsmanship in love, something worthy of her new status, for with the death of Rome she found herself declared nominally free by the scriptures; though the Church fathers went on execrating her, calling her "sovereign pest," "gateway to hell," "arm of the devil," "advance guard of hell," "larva of the demon:" the baleful voices of St John Chrysostom, St Anthony, St Jerome and other Christians of the same outlook. The Roman Empire with its colourful tapestry of nymphs and gods, while poetically satisfying, did nothing to offer woman even a nominal equality of status before the law. The Roman world was completely masculine-inclined and such civic rights as existed were male-dominated in their conception. It is something of a paradox that it was the scriptures which first conferred a new theological freedom on woman — one which she was not slow to accept. When St Paul remarked, "There is neither Jew nor Greek, there is neither bond nor free, there is neither male nor female," he was making place for the new concept of the human "persona," a word which up to then had indicated simply a mask used in stage-plays. In fact it is at this point that one begins to discern the shadow of the ego falling across European thought. In this spread of a Christianity firmly anchored in Jewish monotheism we can read the beginning of the end of a Europe which had still to drag itself through the sterile Dark Ages, the wars and revolutions which would follow each other like the rotation of the seasons. The evangelization of Europe came about largely through the enthusiasm of women, many of whom were queens and princesses, and some of whom became saints or celebrated recluses and anchorites. In an age of decline and dissolution, the Roman world had shattered like a mask, leaving in its place a contradictory mass of beliefs and impulses which were far from presenting a coherent and rounded view of things which the historian of the period might espouse. Consequently there are more questions than answers, and many are the apparent contradictions which he will have to take in his stride if he is to try to bring the age into focus, and most particularly if he wishes to frame Provençal woman and situate her in it on her home ground. Through her the sensibility of Europe was being articulated and shaped, and in her struggle we can see that she was occupied with the right of the woman in terms of love. Courtly love was an entirely original departure, so much so that modern scholarship has shown considerable hesitation in dealing with it. It was set up as a contrast in terms of refinement of sentiment and stylishness of manners to the common-or-garden variety of attachment, a transaction where the woman's role was that of a negotiable chattel merely, who could be bought or bartered by a nobleman in search of offspring or entertainment in his chilly castle.

The most celebrated of these Courts of Love was without any doubt the one which gathered about the illustrious Eleanor of Aquitaine; in fact it has remained the model of the genre. Eleanor, who was in the first place Queen of France and wife of Louis VII, later became Queen of England. Her beauty and amiability were legendary and the poets of the day were not slow to recognize the fact. Her praises were sung by the most famous troubadours, Bernard de Ventadour among them; and even late in life, at sixty years of age, she was still regarded as a paragon of beauty and high style. Her daughter, the Countess Marie de Champagne, by the same token gathered around her in her castle at Troyes an equally brilliant cast of poetic admirers among whom we find the names of Chrétien de Troyes and André le Chapelain: the code of chivalry was quite as exacting as that of the love-code.

The statutes of chivalric behaviour sought to refine and perfect the sentiments which grew up around the exchanges of two hearts expressing themselves in poetry and loving worship. A whole literature has grown up around the practice and precepts of the Code de l'Amour Courtois, and the Courts of Love, with their mock trials and judgements for or against specific cases of love-behaviour, went far to codify social habit and refine morals. In an age so rough and uncouth these mock-trials had a humanizing effect upon the habits and feelings of mere courtiers, as well as insisting upon the female presence as an object of courtly worship. It would be equally true to point out the enriching effect of these literary *tournées* upon poetry and language in general; the Courts of Love were a primitive laboratory where the first of the troubadours elaborated their sentiments in codifying them, and matched words to music in singing the praises of a real-life Muse. In modern times the scholar who has done most work on this blithe subject, and also on the Cathars with their mystical observances, is Dr René Nelli, and it is possible that he has said the last word on the matter. His essays at once so human and so full of insight are themselves full of poetry. For him the love-code enables the sentiment to purify and distil itself by self-abnegation, which seems almost to hint at a kind of Tantric purification of the sort one finds in some of the practices of yoga. The love-sentiment undergoes a process of "crystallization" which requires all the lover's watchful patience. One thing is clear: on the poets of Languedoc and of Aquitaine the influence of Muslim Spain was the most decisive and profound. This at any rate seems to be the mature view of Dr Nelli and he has marshalled an impressive body of evidence to support it; we must bow to the weight of his scholarship. Even Stendhal has borrowed the word "crystallization" from him as a troubadour love-concept, in the pages of *De l'Amour*.

Lawrence Durrell

"But a new age has struck, and a new century! Does the shadow of Romantic Love still hover over modern Provence, or has its basic typology changed?"

Yes, some scholars have tried to give the reality of the Courts of Love a somewhat equivocal appearance but there seems no doubt that they existed in plain fact and were something more than just a courtly amusement to while away the winter boredom of castle life. They provided a rendezvous for high sentiment and high poetry, they helped define both feelings and the young Provençal tongue which was in danger of falling into disrepair from sheer disuse. As a school of manners the Courts were unique, even though so lightly undertaken as befitted a school of philosophic lovers concerned with the glorification of the castle's fair châtelaine. All this was something more than just a courtly parlour game, for it codified courtly behaviour which went far to refine the coarseness of feudal manners and assert the woman's right to be worshipped in appropriate dignity, by fine poetry. The concept was slow to take hold, for it had to make headway against a host of other warring concepts coming from many different quarters and which sought to rush into the vacuum left by the smouldering remnants of a dying paganism. One thinks of extraordinary departures like the Council of Macon (which they warn us is probably apocryphal) at which the Fathers of the Church voted, by a narrow majority, in favour of according woman a soul just like a man! Fair is fair!

The extensive canon of troubadour poetry, by its quality and its prolixity, goes far towards giving the lie to sceptical scholars. The whole business of courtly love was something more than a romantic paradox involving the theatrical factor which has always been so predominant in the Mediterranean spirit. Something deep and pure about the place, the land of Provence, was being expressed by these singular and inventive methods. And best of all, the slumbering language woke to the touch of new music, new words, new passions. Indeed, until this poetry asserted itself, the whole love-transaction was hardly on a higher plane than baronial pig-sticking. Think of the sanguinary louts who spent toilsome lives in bloodshed and pilfering of their neighbours' goods. Philoprogenitive cutpurses with unevolved souls like blood sausage! And then to be accused of not being able to love with dignity and distress!

With the steady dissolution of paganism and the increasingly thorough grasp of the Christian Fathers upon the thought and manners of the epoch, a new woman was born and was able to project a sketch of her nature upon the notions derived from courtly love and its derivatives, in fine poetry and passionate thought-forms in literature. Seen from our vantage-point in history, it seems quite obvious that the only rational occupation for a sane man or woman is to think about love — and to think about it profoundly and continuously, in full tapestry. This is the real aliment of the sensibility, the narrative food of the psyche. But the idea evolved slowly. It had to encounter many prejudices. Provence had its share of philistines, a cumbersome word to indicate men without backs to their heads, or sides to their ideas. Nor is the word "love" used frivolously or licentiously, for the women who were ushering in this new dispensation had realized how to think about love from this new epicentre, a philosophic one. They were walking in the pathways traced by the thought of Plato and Aristotle. Love was a form of metaphysical inquiry and through their poetical thinking the future, as their children would experience it, was enriched and made resonant. And their poets and troubadours and gallants also shared in this influence by proxy. Those who were not boors realized that they also had a poetic duty. They must learn how to accommodate the triple notion of lover, wife and divinity with all the other projections of womanhood, the shadows of which coloured the whole of life and rendered it both rich and various and full of pith. Mother, nurse, muse, despot, slave, confederate, conspirator, worshipper, judge! The charter of love was limitless . . .

One is struck by the dynamism and the capacity for invention which characterizes the new woman. Take, among so many of her kind, a figure like Fabiola, a Roman matron of high society who fell under the spell of St Jerome and became a disciple. Struck by the numbers of pilgrims who came to Rome only to find themselves stranded and without resources, she busied herself with the founding of the first *nosokomeion* or hostel — the original blueprint for a public hospital. Similarly, observing the numbers of pilgrims for the Holy Land who disembarked at Ostia, she founded the first *xenodocheion* or hotel to welcome them (the Greek word means "stranger-receptacle" in the literal sense, for the concept of the hotel was an original one). But before very long all the roads which led to Jerusalem were furnished with their hostels at strategic points. And all this was the inspiration of a single Roman girl who had been swayed by the preaching of St Jerome!

Blue light at dusk

Set me a parody of this small island town
Recalled in silence, birthmark of old memories,
Benchmark of a Roman slave in an oar blade
Not only beautiful but proposing also
To satisfy every human need like church,
Tavern or brothel — blue light at dusk;
Houses of pleasure in coloured bulbs,
Brief as grief but warm as all charity.
Someone born for the inhuman act of love
Between the horns of Minos, yes, pure terror!
Defended by one ikon of her saint,

Provence

"Only a whore," you said: but with the sagacity
Of some great Muse, some great jurist, Marina!
The behaviour of silence is quite artless,
Sleep closing like a door, absolved by kisses.

Yet the smartest and best of the lovers for money
Was Minerva, secret of her freshness the two
Musk-melons kept between her thighs in summer,
Keeping cool as spice the human fruit — ourselves
Engendered love in silence like a young polar
Cleopatra gone to seed, yet garnered sigh by sigh.
To humour the dead in August when you die most;
Detectives of the worthless human kiss,
Your currency of love must end like this,
Blue grief at dusk and some quiet love
At cockcrow with the ruins of the sky.

At any rate the Courts of Love had a distinctly educational function: it was lion-taming on a grand scale, and also a declaration of the aristocracy of fine literature. Vulgar serfs and shopkeepers would be too devoured by the pains and stresses of ordinary life to think much further than the daily needs of bed and board. Courtly love, as it evolved under the finer touches of the poetic sensibility, insisted on sentiment as the *gai savoir* of the Happy Few. Stendhal recognized the terrain at once when he hit the Midi and heard the bells of Avignon. But of course all this must have been there, under the surface; it did not evolve in a night. Most important of all, the language with its supple accents and its values firmly planted in the plainsong of the human heart, was ready and waiting for its troubadours. But they were a motley and un-predictable lot and the weird polarity of their feelings some-times strikes a chill where it should thrill. Absolute passions could come to grief by their very excess, and sometimes the historian has been led astray by a striving for false effects, even such a scrupulous apologist as J. A. Symonds, who sketches the career of Fouquet, so celebrated in his time as a love-poet, in the following words: "The gentle melodist whom Dante placed in Paradise, served Adelaisie, wife of Bérald, with long service of unhappy love, and wrote upon her death, 'The Complaint of Bérald des Baux for his Adelaisie.' " But the reality was somewhat different, for this Fouquet was so overcome with sorrow that he became a monk of Citeau upon the death of his lady and finally rose to be Bishop of Marseille and lastly Archbishop of Toulouse. In this, his last role, his innate fanaticism seems to have come to the surface for

"in his dealings with the Albigenses he exercised the ferocity of a wolf. There was no act of treachery or cruelty throughout the war in which he was not the most forward, sanguinary and unscrupulous. Having given half his life to gallantry he then gave up without restraint to the cause of tyranny, murder and spoliation, and most unhappily he profited by it . . . Loving women passionately, a quite ferocious apostle of the Inquisition, he did not give up the composition of verses which bore the impress of his successive passions."

Another celebrated poet in the same galaxy was William de Cabestanh, who sang the praises of Berengaria des Baux. But time passed and the poet's heart proved itself somewhat fickle: he switched his attentions to the lovelier Sermonda, wife of the hot-blooded Raymond de Roussillon, who registered his distaste for this romantic spooning in a characteristic and imaginative burst of irritation: he waylaid and slew the troubadour and cut out his heart, which he instructed his chef to serve up for dinner that night. Unwittingly his wife partook of a portion and was then informed that she had supped on her lover's heart; she was so horrified that she threw herself from the highest window in the castle, and was dashed to pieces on the crags below. This outrage was the occasion of a civil war, for the relatives of Sermonda and William de Cabestanh appealed for revenge to Alphonso, King of Aragon, who responded by invading the territories of the Count of Roussillon *à la maraude* with his army of freebooters, putting everything and everyone to the test of fire and sword. An awkward business, which I quote only to illustrate the chancy nature of human relationships among these slightly unhinged poets of love and their Muses.

But there is quite enough evidence of the weight and imaginative power of the Courts of Love to allow us to take them seriously. Moreover, true love also flourished and overrode mere snobbery, for at least two members of the princely family were proud to adopt the profession themselves, Bernard des Baux in the twelfth century and in the next Rambaud des Baux. And then of course the overshadowing weight of Dante and Petrarch illustrates clearly that the human sensibility was hungry for a new approach to love and to the woman's role.

"The Courts of Love were originally courts in which the rules of minstrelsy were laid down, they pronounced on the qualifications of a candidate, they polished and cherished the Langue d'Oc in its purity, dictated the subjects upon which the troubadours were to compose their lays, judged their pretensions, settled their controversies, recompensed their merits and punished by disgrace or exclusion those who violated the laws. In the twelfth century these Courts of Ladies drew up Provençal grammars in which the rules of the dialect were laid down . . . But these Courts of Love went further. They laid down rules for love; they allowed married women to receive the homage of lovers, and even nicely directed all the symptoms they were to exhibit of reciprocation" (S. Baring-Gould in 1891).

But this rather shocked Victorian parson then writes off the whole business as a time-killing "solemn fooling." A grievous error in my view, even though the historic evidence is very various and one can prove almost anything one wants in this business.

*   *   *

Reflecting on these matters brings to mind Marie and her unfinished manuscript. For some time after her death in Naxos the words "death" and "Sicily" began to co-exist in my mind as if they had always belonged together, yoked like husband and wife. This strange binary thought or feeling took on a kind of poetic reality by association when certain vectors of memory asserted themselves: the slopes and valleys of verdant corners of Cyprus, lying in deep grass. For her, purely in friendship, I ad-libbed my way through the three-volume autobiography of the man whose friendship she most esteemed, Maurice Chevalier. Her French was not quite up to the task and she was an impatient as well as beautiful soul. It gave me a glimpse of what even then I recognized as the courtly love of Provençal vintage. So old and so sincere an attachment was equal to all the constraints of age and distance and war-provoked silences. The sentiment was pure gold, drenched in the piety and the prudence of affectionate reticence. And then in later years to come to the scene of our last happy meetings in Avignon, our last farewell, for we did not recognize death walking towards us — one never does! But I knew the measure of her love because once she woke me long after midnight with a phone call, arriving almost at once in a taxi with a bottle of champagne and flowers to tell me: "Darling, Anaïs is dead. I didn't want you to hear the news from anyone but me."

Style in loving!

We were so confident about seeing each other again during the coming summer we never gave the matter a thought. Indeed a few days before her death the phone rang in this silent house and picking it up I heard what sounded like the waves hissing on her beach at Naxos. Then her familiar voice with its calm enduring youthfulness, the little speech-halt on the "r" so that I was always "Law-wence." We planned to meet in Rome and visit Sicily together (I had never been there then). We also spoke of Provence, I recall, and her projected manuscript. The thread she was following was a romantic poem, now long forgotten but then in high fashion, called *The Eaten Heart* by Richard Aldington, which was built around the tragedy of Cabestanh and was the work of a thoroughly pre-Raphaelite sensibility. We proposed to spend a whole winter studying the troubadours and their history. Something might emerge from it, we thought. But it was not to be as we planned it.

I was happy to be reminded that for one of her birthdays I managed to find her an old recording of her cavalier of the heart singing his famous "Louise" with all his magical impertinence and tenderness. In Cyprus. In the shadow of the ancient Abbey of Bellapaix.

Yes, Denis de Rougemont was right when he said that the heart of any book about Provence would be the history of modern love: perhaps Meredith would be one's poet then? He would certainly appreciate the sort of romantic panache one encounters even today under the trivialized behaviour of so many ordinary souls. I recall that when Catha Aldington married her taurine husband Jacques, who raised fighting bulls in the Camargue, she was not at all surprised when he rode away for a weekend and disappeared from sight. When he returned, he explained that he had gone to Avignon to hunt for the works of Shakespeare, "because it would be unthinkable to marry a girl without knowing her national poetry, her heart!" Nobody seemed to think there was anything unusual about such a sentiment. In Provence they somehow unconsciously believe that sincere loving polishes and perfects souls, just as they still believe that the eyes are the seat of the soul, whence the peasant saying "Anyone can make a child *mais il faut parfaire les yeux.*" The young may feel disposed to mock these romantic attitudes, but after the excesses of the sixties and seventies, there are some who have seen the Provençal light, and are reverting to a belief in fine style for loving.

"But the real temper of this fierce tribe was not shown among troubadours, or in the courts of love and beauty. The stern and barren rock from which they sprang and the comet of their scutcheon, are the true symbols of their nature. History records no end of their ravages and slaughters. It is a tedious catalogue of blood . . . There is nothing terrible, splendid, and savage, belonging to feudal history, of which an example may not be found in the annals of Les Baux, as narrated by their chronicler Jules Canonge" (J.A. Symonds).

Yes, this was the unlikely human material upon which our fine ladies went to work to try to coax a semblance of culture and grace from the brutal hearts of these feudal chieftains. That a fine poetry found its source-book here in this blood-curdling fastness, and others like it, is a tribute to their own high intuitions and graces. Not all these romantic fictions were just rhetoric, as their biographies show us. Some attachments were based on passions which proved fatal. But how to resist their names?

In 1244, the troubadours vied with each other in lauding Cecilia des Baux, whom they christened Passerose because of her exceptional beauty. Other beauties, all from the same family, were Clairette and Etiennette de Ganteaume, and Baussette, the daughter of Hugh des Baux, celebrated by Roger of Arles. We must not forget that the satirical Cervantes pilloried this version of courtly love in his "peerless" Dulcinea de Toboso, but I am inclined to believe the basic coarseness of the Spanish character, with its deep yet suppressed hatred of woman, was responsible — the writer missed the point of the Provençal invention — but not Dante, not Petrarch! Another sinner was the cheeky King René of Anjou who was quite a hand at distributing savage nicknames which stuck. He masterminded such unflattering designations as Inconstance des Baux, Déloyauté de Beaufort, Envie de Candole, Dissolution de Castelane, Sottise de Grasse and Opiniâtreté de Sade . . . One wonders what he did for friends!

But of course, as de Rougemont has reminded us, the only real danger is insincerity and affectation, enemies of the human heart. Yet I recall someone saying, "If I were a man I would be a trifle dubious about girls with such fantastically lovely names lest they turned into Proust's chauffeur on closer acquaintance!"

The master key to the whole subject of courtly love is *L'Art d'Aimer*, a manuscript in the Bibliothèque Nationale (Lat 8748). This is a handsome parchment of the fourteenth century in an excellent state of preservation, and the text, with variants, has been often reprinted. It obviously owes a good deal to Ovid (*Ars Amatoria*), as most mediaeval writing of the same period does, but the difference is that Ovid concentrated on titillation whereas this . . . it is not on the same vector at all, though it uses the same source material. We know nothing about its author save his name and the fact that he was a churchman, and even a chaplain; the last fact is striking since it might indicate that he was the private chaplain to someone exalted like the Queen of France, or Pope Innocent IV. The little book is a serious and exhaustive study of its subject, and is dedicated to one Gauthier who is described as being "désireux de servir dans la Chevalerie d' Amour," a kind of confraternity of courtly lovers dedicated to this science of happiness. It is concerned with the topic of love viewed as an art. Yes, *L'Art d'Aimer* of André Le Chapelain is the dictionary of courtly love as it was viewed by the great ladies who presided at the Courts of Love, as well as the troubadours whose songs illustrated the loves which were in question, in judgement. Their value was judged by the fair jury of great ladies and a verdict brought in upon the case in question: did it figure in terms of the agreed Code of Courtly Love? The little treatise mentions a number of trials and a number of verdicts upon examples of gallantry, and one is struck to see the names of eminent society figures emerging from his texts: "Seven for the Countess of Champagne, seven for the Lady Ermengarde of Narbonne, three from Queen Eleanor, three from the Queen of France and two from the Countess of Flanders." It gives fair weight to a belief in the existence of these assizes of Courtly Love.

But what of the actual Code of Conduct?

It is not dogmatic but hortatory: it seeks to invoke a courtly disposition in the subject, and it stresses all the human virtues as being desirable and fruitful in the lover by intent. Chapter Three of the treatise presents them in the form of two lists, a shorter divided into thirteen precepts and a longer numbering thirty-one "laws." They are translated in full here from the French text of Le Chapelain because they give a kind of sketch of the courtly philosophy and the ideal type of disposition desirable in the lover. They are also interesting as a commentary on the morals of the twelfth century. Perhaps this little book of rules might intrigue the modern reader as a psychology in little.

Principal Precepts of Love

1. Avoid all avarice like the plague; on the contrary, practise liberality
2. Don't tell lies
3. Don't backbite
4. Don't divulge the secrets of lovers
5. Don't confide your love to too many people
6. Keep yourself pure for your lover
7. Don't consciously seek to derail the love of another

8. Don't seek the love of someone you would be ashamed to marry
9. Be attentive to all commands emanating from the order of chivalry in love
10. Try always to be worthy to belong to the order of chivalry in love
11. In every circumstance be polite and courteous
12. In giving yourself up to the pleasures of love never exceed the desires of your lover
13. Whether giving or receiving pleasure in lovemaking always keep a certain native shyness of attitude

This is only the opening statement; it is followed by a further chapter, longer and more detailed, which sets out thirty-one further precepts. For the sake of completeness I add them here, translating them from the French.

The Rules of Lovecraft

1. The pretext of marriage is not a justifiable excuse against the rights of love
2. Lovers who feel no jealousy cannot really love
3. Nobody should have two love affairs at the same time
4. Love is always increasing or diminishing by its nature
5. There is no delight in what is obtained against the wishes of the loved one
6. Man can only really love after puberty
7. After the death of the beloved the survivor should wait two years
8. Nobody should be deprived of the object of his passion without good reason
9. Nobody really loves without fair hopes of reciprocity

10. True love flees a house of avarice like the plague
11. One should not love someone one would be ashamed to marry
12. The complete lover desires only the kisses of the beloved and of no one else
13. A love which is too much confided to others rarely lasts
14. An easy conquest renders a love valueless, but a difficult one increases its value
15. All lovers should turn pale in the presence of the beloved
16. The unexpected glimpse of the beloved should make the lover's heart falter
17. A new love chases away the old
18. Merit alone renders love worthy of the lover
19. Diminishing love fades fast and seldom recovers its strength
20. The lover is always fearful
21. A truthful jealousy increases love
22. At a single doubt cast upon a lover, jealousy and desire both increase
23. He who is eaten up by his passion neither eats nor sleeps
24. Whatever the lover's act it finds its dwelling in the thought of the beloved
25. A true lover approves nothing that the beloved does not like
26. The lover refuses nothing to his beloved
27. The true lover can never be sated of the pleasures of the beloved
28. The smallest presumption of turpitude about the lover pushes the lover to fear the worst about the beloved
29. He who possesses too great luxury does not love well
30. The true lover is continuously plunged in the image of the beloved
31. There is nothing to prevent a woman being loved by two men, nor a man being loved by two fair women

It does not seem very all-inclusive or even penetrating, yet if the strategy was to try and create a virtuous disposition in the baron of the twelfth century, one can see the force of the argument and the direction it is taking. My examples, both texts and opinions, come from the admirable monograph of J. Lafitte Houssat, *Troubadours et Cours d'amour*.

I do not think that my view of old Provence as a sort of crucible in which the European sensibility forged itself anew is exaggerated. It was here and nowhere else that the relationship of human love and divine was elaborated and examined in depth, later to evolve itself further in terms of philosophy and literature. The seed-bed for human values was in this fruitful and disconcerting landscape which has managed to combine such dissimilar preoccupations as courtly love on the one hand and alchemy on the other. Was there ever such a range of topics discussed in so modest a space? While witchcraft and black magic flourished in the high Cevennes, the Cabala was being elaborated in Vauvert and the science of medicine made Montpellier a world-renowned centre of the healing arts!

Consequently, these matters are worth the attention of the modern traveller who finds himself receiving the magnetic waves off the land through which he is travelling: a patchwork quilt of a hundred colours. It is the right place to re-read your Ovid and compare his pleasantly salacious views about sex — his savage archness — with the later Provençal views which had become tinged with the mystical transcendence of the Dantean vision. The pure and disembodied love of Petrarch for Laura was surely another kind of animal?

It was Petrarch who first decided that Provence was for a great poet the love-box of history. Nothing exceeds in magic his description of Laura — her star-spangled robe, her eyes like thrifty amethysts ablaze, her astonished silence before the realization that things could go no further. It was he! At last! She did not need to hear his voice. A single look spelled out the whole praxis of poetic love between them. She was dying to get away from him to examine her feelings; as for him, he was faint with exultation — he had to lean against a wall in Avignon. Not a word was said at this momentous happening.

But he had discovered a principle of great importance for his happiness (and hers), namely that death is not negotiable except through poetry and that language was really inadequate to subsume truth. Yet the existential human sorrow which reigned when one realized this enabled one to circumvent despair. How beautiful and how relevant the biography of Petrarch in its religious coherence! The long journeys to feed and refresh the imagination, impregnated by mountains like Ventoux and Aigoual, plus the long periods of debauch and horror before which he was helpless. She accepted it because she knew its inner tantric significance. Nature was just a divine prank. They made physical love very rarely — afraid of so much intensity — afraid of lying in each other's arms!

Statue of lovers: Aix

Roasts on in ageless loneliness, the sage,
All but abandoned by his very sex,
With no such drastic animals to keep
At bay, allows his dreams to vex:
Is troubled by young daikinis in his sleep!

In France poor sputtering Sade presides
On love and smears the wench of time
By tedious repetition — dulls;
Of all experiences the one sublime
(The silent kiss the mortuary confines).

But no dissection could as well describe
The science of this woman's head, the beauty,
Eaten away by siege, by time, by fire,
(Young sorrows incubate in man's desire)
Like sonnets engendered by the rain
Beating on some old poet's hat,
The psyche's pious dimorphism means just that —
Her kiss may never strike again!

I recall a journey we made once, long ago, in which these matters formed the staple of our conversation. The weather was breaking, it was autumn and the harvest had been an exceptionally rich one. Someone — I suppose it was Aldo — had suggested that we embark on horseback and ride from St-Rémy across the chalk plain, around the Alpilles and northward as far as the Vaucluse, the spring so dear to Petrarch. It was to be a sort of peripatetic journey of inquiry into the natural origins of Provençal love. We had not forgotten, you see, that the route would lead us past that other melancholy monument to love — the tantrism of the left hand, so to speak — at Lacoste: the ruined château of the Marquis de Sade.

Everything conspired to render the whole experience as characteristically miserable as a reading of the works of Sade, for the rain burst its banks, so to speak, and literally seethed among the woods. We tried to solace ourselves with an inadequate cassoulet and a wine of poor contrivance. Perhaps my rather acid view of the Marquis is in part due to this inadequate fare, but truth to tell, the history of Lacoste is a sad one, a history of sieges, persecutions, rape, galleys . . .

Extremes meet, they say, and on this journey we were disposed to see Sade and Petrarch in this light. Aristotle: Plato! Freud: Jung! The heart's eternal dispute with itself . . . In recent years there has been some tendency to build the ungallant Marquis into a natural philosopher of sorts, responsible for some sort of intellectual judgement upon the world of his time. But he was rather a shallow specimen of libertine and intellectual coxcomb. A poor stylist and a pitiable dramatist. And I should accuse him of lacking both humour and humanity. Still, it is intriguing that a relative of the libertine, Hugues de Sade, a son of a syndic of Avignon, married Laure de Noves, the Laura of Petrarch, while the definitive biography of the poet is by the hand of another member of the Sade family: an abbé de Sade no less. In the inventory of our libertine's library the three volumes of the biography "voisinent avec des productions libertines" (lie cheek by jowl with pornographic works).

And there are some intriguing ironies in the history of Lacoste by Henri Fauville. Such as: "In the eyes of Sade, sexual liberty was a right — a right denied to the lower classes." But sometimes he poses as a champion of traditional morality, especially when infractions risk involving him in a loss of money! This is illustrated by a quote from a letter to Gaufridy where de Sade says, "I made that little bitch Madelon appear before me and I assured her that it was she who gave André the clap and if she did not at once take steps to pay for his cure I would have her drummed out of the village."

The ruined château, its bare spars spread to heaven, is a sad relic; and of course its obscene and grim associations of child murders and violations cannot help but colour one's impressions. All this by a repugnant frail moonlight and orchestrated by the squelch of saddles which the rain had rendered heavy and sopping.

Yet the next day everything had changed for the better, the sky cleared, the sun came out and with it our spirits revived and the romantic charm of our journey seemed to blossom anew as we came riding into Avignon in a blazing sunset to cast anchor in the little courtyard of the Hôtel d'Europe, fully assured of a fair welcome. We were to lie here for the night before pushing on down to the Fountain of Vaucluse to pay respects to Laura and her poet: from the profane to the sacred! Meanwhile, among the convivialities of dinner Aldo found time to read his favourite travel-guide Augustus Hare, and ask us to admire his chapter on Avignon, scrupulous and accurate work indeed.

"Scarcely anything remains of the ancient Avenio, except a few stones built into the walls and some mosaics in the museum. The remains of the rule of the Popes are magnificent. At Avignon the traveller will first feel himself in the south: its crenellated walls and machicolated towers rise from a country covered with olives, though laden with white dust and swept by a bitter mistral. This wind, the scourge of the country, is supposed to keep the town healthy . . . Men, brown and tanned, walk with their jackets slung over their shoulders. In summer, numbers of the people sleep in the streets, the dwelling open to all the world."

The night was made deeply impressive by the ghostly silhouettes of the bastions, and there was a light in the little tomb-shrine of St Bénézet on the famous broken bridge which once was to unite Provence with the secret rugged dissenting reaches of Languedoc. Only four of its twenty-two arches remain today.

By the following afternoon we at last reached the celebrated fountain, the Sorgue's ample source. The water gushes with unimaginable abundance and freshness through the verdant yet secretive valleys, falling down upon a precipitous limestone cliff into a deep black pool, luminous and noisy, whence in smaller thunderous leaps it descends to a rich limestone valley. The air is rich with water. The rocks are crowned by a ruin called the Château de Pétrarque. It was, however, to a villa in the valley that the poet retired in 1337, having been deeply impressed by the atmosphere of the place after a childhood visit in 1313. It was here, he says, that all his work was either executed, begun or conceived. He would never have left the spot, he goes on to narrate, had he not by strange chance received on the same day two letters: one summoning him to Rome, signed by the Senate, and one from Paris from the chancellor: they summoned him to receive the poetic crown of olive as supreme laureate. This was for his poem "Africa," on the Punic Wars. He chose Rome and was crowned on the Capitol in April 1341.

It would be over-imaginative to conjure up traces of the absent image of Laura here, though the place breathes the very spirit of peace and concentration. The dark water makes its own characteristic music, and the air is full of the singing of nightingales while, in the shadowy glades over the pool, there were roses in bloom. In the shade of a willow we drank a toast to an invisible presence; but nobody spoke, and it was in silence that we turned and rode away.

Conclusion: *Le cercle refermé*

Cunégonde or,
Memoirs of the little French bidet

Aldo's letter came after such a long separation from Provence that I hardly dared to respond to the invitation of my old friend. He challenged me to join him for a "Provençal water party" somewhere between Avignon and Narbonne, on the most companionable though most treacherous of rivers, the Rhône. In summer, in fine weather, yes, with the chance of renewing old friendships which absence was throwing into disrepair. Moreover, this was to be in the company of Cunégonde, the last pupil of the philosopher Demonax. Everyone adored her though nobody could say exactly why, except that like so many philosophers there was a touch of the preposterous about her. Her name was that of Voltaire's favourite niece. I had already hinted that my last travel-book would be for her, dedicated to her, half-paragon and half-witch, initiate and symbol. Yes.

In fact she turned out to be a Latex doll of great beauty, resilience and simplicity. For a while she even seemed a bit strange and equivocal — until you realized her superiority over a real woman, a woman of the flesh. For she was totally submissive. Her warmth and peristalsis were secured by electricity and she was denied all possibility of answering back. It was perfection! Sapient Cunégonde! She rejoiced in real power, i.e. silence.

Satyrikon — Visitor's Book

My notion was to revive the Satyrikon as a birthday present to myself and fill the banqueting hall of the château with candlelight, in honour of the guests of Petronius. They were all so anxious to make the acquaintance of my Latex phantom that they came early, to the intense delight of little Cunégonde herself. Of course she had much to explain, if not to excuse, for normally women of her kind are conceived in heaven, not made on earth. But in her case the answer was agency work. When first she met Petronius she had been running a matrimonial agency for men too old to care. It was not always completely convincing. In fact one poet described it as trying to sanctify Swiss cock-teasing with intellectual high-mindedness, to the distress of all truthful persons. Old P. insisted on a high intellectual tone.

"After the fatal explosion it took some years for the fall-out to settle and for the volcanoes to heal themselves by seepage; it was impossible to judge the rate at which matter became habitable once more — perhaps never? It was time which I spent holed up in an old-style island château on the rim of the Santorin crater, preparing the way for a book which would describe man's new estate in a world which I provisionally called Moribundia. The island travelled through a rain of ashes and utter darkness, punctuated from time to time by an explosion of hot slag and embers the size of skyscrapers. Time we spent hidden in the labyrinth of caves which honeycombed the island. Impossible to predict our survival rate: from the way things were developing it looked as if everything must be done all over again, starting from scratch, everything created anew with 'let there be light!'

"The rain of ashes consisted of burnt pages of world literature, fragments of poems and novels, the sum total of human knowledge, the gigantic cast which decorated world history and populated the chronicles of empires: Gods, empresses, eunuchs and ghosts, poets and prophets, defying the laws of consequence and sense. What was to be done?

"Among others Dr Sinclair came to me in a dream, all ready to inhabit a book which I had not yet written. The confident stride, the top hat and frock coat, the copious dyed moustache which he could blow out with a jubilant 'ffff.' The piety and care with which he put them down, stethoscope and top hat. There he sat, slightly pop-eyed but calm as a Roman emperor, completely certain of his ground. His silences were as magistral as they were penetrating. Then came the strategic moment of the huge diagnosis when with an air of superhuman certainty he blew out his cheeks and his moustaches with them and uttered the single word: 'Worms!'' And so it always proved to be! We passed them, the said worms, thanks to his decoction of wormwood and arsenic — left over from a depleted medicine chest which dated from before the flood — in an age when Utter Moribundia had not been created. Dr Sinclair treated everyone with fear or favour. Yes, all the characters in all the novels flocked to his consultations, finding them invigorating. One day they would be able to announce with a flourish, 'Today, I passed the head.' And the Doctor would smile and say, 'I somehow guessed you had from your expression at lunch!' They were many, his clients, and very various as to type and avocation. The high technology of the little Swiss miss from Geneva, wound up like a watch into a state of pure irresistibility like a beehive on holiday. Then Marie-Marie's huge favourite, the blackamoor with a sperm count of 112. It was rumoured that he could see around corners because he had one glass eye which was blue and could be taken out. She spoke of his titanic member gushing love. There was her spasmodic Turk called Yusuf Al Masri, as well as Spoke the Druid who got drunk on Embalming Fluid. Sinclair sighed his 'ffff' sigh and said, 'It takes all sorts to unmake a world, *n'est-ce pas?*' Old Davidov was a Visigoth with a simple but truthful wig. Other outside personages from other novels sometimes dropped in, like Mrs Trinc-Nombril, the ideal *femme d'intérieur*, described by Professor Quibble as 'une fille à toute épreuve.' His own girlfriend was the little redskin they called Mouchoir, a swarthy slave mistress with a honeyed glance.

"Admiral Skipaheartbeat kept watch and ward over our potations, for we had been left by fate the stocks of rum and other beverages destined for the Mediterranean Fleet. And candles! Everything centred on the candles which we lit at night before pouring out our drinks. The Admiral affected full dress uniform for the event — dazzling white duck with medals straight out of the *arrière-boutique* of a Ptolemy. It turned the whites of his eyes to pearl.

"There were others, like Madame Vesuvius who organized her little team of slithering Jewesses, athirst for gold, into contemporary groupings according to the language they spoke. She still had a little bit of the Japanese love-gargle for which she had become celebrated. The girls were in full splendour — how well one knew the smile! The smile of a king-cobra floating in formol!

"As for Socrates, once so gifted for friendship and dispute, he has put away his intellectual toys. They carried him dying into the house, but on a sudden impulse he had them stop under an olive to refresh himself with a heartbeat of human wine. In truth he wanted for one last brief moment to hear the mysterious Voice which had come to inhabit his sleep and which he hoped would gather up and summarize all his various intuitions and findings in coherent form and order. The winter had been particularly hard that year of recorded time — imagine frost in January with a temperature of as much as minus twenty for a month or more. Birds died on the branch, frozen stiff; sentries died in their hoods hanging upon the barbed wire of forgotten battlegrounds. They will fall with the first snap-thaw like ripe fruit, death-ripened fruit. Makes you think that we shall all end like this — just a stain in the snow. I can recall Carmen saying, 'Do you remember when you insisted on paying me before making love? I found it exciting, yes. That was in Avignon. I think at heart every girl wants to be paid!' "

*   *   *

When I rang the rusty mediaeval chime of the château, Aldo himself came hurrying down to greet me, asking eagerly all the while, "Is she with you? Have you got her, Cunégonde?" And there she was, sitting bolt upright in the back of the great car, looking about her as if she had woken from sleep. "A beautiful tomcat smelling fresh fish!" A Ptolemaic sculpture!

Cunégonde was everything but a wife, yet she was the other kind of person — a mimic of faultless intention. The Latex image fulfilled the promptings of her rubber heart. It was cupboard love with a vengeance. Her marvellous perfected body cast no shadow. The bewitching smile was a superb free accessory to a love full of whispered conversations. The rubber confessions of the perfect woman ("Going into production soon!"). The philosophic truths which abounded she called "Mnemons," after her master, Demonax.

When I first saw her she was clad in the magnificent car she had bought for herself in Avignon — all gunmetal and cream and mirrors and a mink interior worthy of the great actress she turned out to be. She wore a silk shift with "The original Japanese nightingale" embroidered on it, while on her back in pearls ran the legend "Total submission! Yes, I mean it!". There were nevertheless some intriguing prohibitions in her culture, for example she was not allowed to utter the word "Mother" without written permission. Why? But my friends were enthralled by her, and quite specially by her laughter, its indolence and its suggestion of a hidden gravity, while I myself grew suddenly afraid of so much beauty entrusted to my keeping. I suddenly realized with her (I was not the only one) that I had never loved anyone. I grew ashamed as I watched her beauty unroll before me: watched with the vigilance of a keeper watching over a lion or a precious snake. I felt doomed.

And seeing my scared face she said, "You don't need to speak to me, just think at me and I will answer whatever passes in your thoughts." And then came the laughter which broke the heart! She was not a person, but an experience — who nowadays is?

Yes, if you go in search of Cunégonde you can hardly forbear to find her. But you must search in all the right places. Myself I was hoping that, thanks to Demonax, she had hoarded a few fragments of the ancient logic which (they promised) would put humanity (meaning me!) back on the right vector and open a window on the holy rainbow of sin and its meanings.

But it was like trying to track down the Golden Fleece from an obscure carbon-dating on a volcanic shard! I told Aldo: "All I know is that she is as beautiful as she is callipygous, fatally factitious and fortuitous to the view. You will find her sitting alone on a rock in the middle of the ocean, waiting for life to subside and renew itself in the volcanic crater of Santorin, say, and all the while making fugitive notes on a wax tablet." It is very moving to the scientific mind. Here is someone I could love . . . you feel it but stifle the thought.

The laughter was a kind of spiritual afterthought. She drew it from a fountain of undefiled visibility which wells eternally from the heart of the cryptic volcano engendered in the human heart by time and the whole theory of change — the mutation harboured by human kisses at their most subtle — that is to say, unpremeditated, fed by a hermetic lust, real time! Pure duration.

She herself explained it by saying, "I know God loves me and I also know why. It is because I am completely unprincipled." On another occasion she added, "Human love is based on thrift. As a good Jewess I study the cash-flow of my lovers. Only thus can one count the dimples in the Creator's chin." I had written to Aldo expressing my misgivings. "Sometimes I feel I am going mad when I realize she is not real but fashioned in Latex. If not 'real,' what is she in truth, then? The philosophic dilemma of all time!" Aldo from his fortress with all its keeps and hidden laboratories and fastnesses replied laconically, "If you had her as a reality would you still want her — alive and breathing, so to speak? Surely it is her singularity which charms and seduces, her relation to a rubber suicide-kit? An investment in rubber?" But it was easy to talk like this when you were not face to face with her. Those eyes! She was, in the most literal sense, too good to be true.

> *Cunégonde his only love,*
> *(As below, so above)*
> *A bivouac in every bed*
> *With sighs enough to wake the dead*
>
> *Battle with inadvertent love*
> *"As below also above"*
> *Cunégonde will see you through,*
> *Do not tell her what to do,*
> *She's the original, whom from whom,*
> *Loving was woven on her loom,*
> *Lead her smiling to the tomb.*

Lawrence Durrell

When Cunégonde started to fall in love it caused much laughter — the holy pruritus of the sublime attachment. "People say you can get rich this way — rubber makes rich!" They tried to convince her that the Turks had thicker foreskins than Christians. For them, love was no drudgery. Listen! You can hear the mandolins pining in nightclubs of a baleful charm, the old caresses have an intravenous appeal which gives drink to the thirsty without undue alarm.

> *My last love was a smiling cramp*
> *She sped the poetry with a gamp,*
> *The coffin was another story,*
> *I wanted nacre for the glory.*
> *Something, I mean, that never fades —*
> *But all they gave me was the "AIDS."*

Another admonition of Demonax which Cunégonde was fond of quoting concerned conduct — the conduct which one got from yoga. "Try and make everything seem inadverted, fortuitous, given, spontaneous, yet secretly will. Only the impossible is worth thinking of as an objective. Believe me, I know it!" But then he added on a depressive note, "There is no reason for things to be as they are. As a poet I am dying of blood-poisoning, for I know that it is fatal for my art for me to preach: yet, I must." This was all very well for someone so given to preaching with the sword.

> *The No Balls Prize for English Lit.*
> *Was given to a perfect fit*
> *Professor Tangboom filled the bill,*
> *Expressions of the human will,*
> *A drunken comet pissing fire*
> *Could illustrate his heart's desire.*

"Confessio ad Absurdum! How many of you understand the Oxherding Drawings? A lama told me that they were nature's primordial message, namely, 'Don't push, just wait and wish.' Provence is full of 'stashes' — a stash is a lay-by for perishable plunder. Thus spake Cunégonde: 'Nothing is so bad that it couldn't get just that little bit worse. Mark my words. Regard yourself as a privileged person drinking nectar on the sly from a sieve. Love lives on leftovers, benign as an elephant in a hammock of roses. The Ministry of Pulp has been such a help, with its nightgowns full of excrement and jovial godmichets.' Cunégonde laughs and claps her hands: 'See! I am real,' she says, and we all agree.

"From a baby upwards towards this leaden coffin the die was cast by fate, I was born bored, was possessed by an insurmountable aristocratic fever of disdain. All the ruins of sameness welled up between the kisses and one knows oneself to be working for Smithereens Incorporated, vowed to the genetic fever of ruin which must beset the race."

> *A Bogomil in love, a Visigoth in sex,*
> *The existential sorrow*
> *Was surely made to vex.*

The candlelit barges sliding down the river with the dinner guests of old P. Cunégonde had never seen anything so bathed in beauty — the water, the light, the flights of birds against a velvet sky. Dining on slices of cold hyena they glide downriver past Avignon. They make a noise like a liquid conspiracy of Chinese paperweights. They spoke of love without an owner, masterless loves in silence, loitering loves, sifted through silences of meditation, until at last Arbiter broke the silence to proclaim some item of poetic truth such as: "The true elephant can fan its wife with its ears, even abbreviate its death by music — often for years."

But of course the great secret of Provence has always been love and its history, and we were very conscious of the fact as we travelled down the river with all its memories. Haunted by the vast allegories which were evoked by names like Petrarch and Laura, Caesar and Cleopatra, love sacred as well as profane, Cunégonde led us to them and enabled us to see them in all their poetic and philosophic depth.

The real original was, of course, Caesar, whose vast ghost still haunts the precincts of the Languedoc with its castles and gloomy keeps, its waterways and green solitudes with solitary swans and geese lying on them in gem-like meditation. When someone wrote, "La Provence, lieu de la haute magie et de la sorcellerie," he was really thinking of Roman Provence, roughly the towns which fall into the provenance of Arles, Avignon, Narbonne and the rest. The other Provence is the one of mountains and caves, of glaciated rocks scored by secret rivers, places scant in folklore where the wild boars still roved and where the golden eagles gyred and swerved above the groves of laurel and cypress. "Places," said Aldo, "where a man could hear himself think *enfin*: where he was in no danger of being killed by a flying champagne cork as might be the case in Nîmes, Avignon, Montpellier and such-like Romanized places!"

They were cut out for the tourist trade, to realize themselves as health spas, while our own Provence was a place of revelations. So we liked to think, a land impossible to sum up with any ease or finality. The waters could swallow it without an afterthought if they wished. (Witness the disastrous and unexpected floods in the centre of Nîmes in 1988, with the houses bent like bows under the water, the great arenas filling up like a kettle under the onslaught. And more astonishing still, the motor-cars hanging in the trees like strange fruit, while by the Maison Carrée I saw two concert grands slowly floating off downstream bound for the underground caves and bunkers which served the eastern end of the town as a parking area. And the noise of the water — like the blundering tread of a herd of wild elephants on the march, even to the snorting and trumpeting . . .)

*   *   *

187

Provence

"When Tiberius lost all his teeth at last, the Imperial Chewer was invoked to help — to chew and spit into the holy mouth: proud of the honour, though the menu was such gloomy fare: at last he grew bored, ordered a change of air, with caviare and wine at each repast, the servant grew quite tipsy at the last. And poetry, need I add, primed the convivial souls — read aloud by famous actors by candlelight beside a dead body in a shroud: a recent gladiator's body, as an *aide-mémoire* explained, 'Why, old emperors must dream aloud, having no other way to raise the dead. Give us this day our chewer's daily bread.'

"Arbiter has discovered that poetry is more than a technique of psychic appraisal for those who recognize the force of breath. It is also a school of virtue which subsumes careless vice. He says that the modern maker has become a lackey, always on the look-out for a handout from some university.

"Now we are told that the complete time-span of the viewer's or reader's attention is only three minutes before he switches to a fresh channel. Poor poets, poor poetry. They look ashamed because they know that their poltroonery is keeping lazy dons in business. No wonder that more and more are opting out.

"Arbiter used to say that everything started to go wrong when he was governor general in Bithynia. Here he first heard the word 'socialism' and experienced the revolt of the slaves at first hand. Quite impossible to evaluate what it did to the Roman soul, the Roman heart. Coarseness of vision was installed as a norm. We began to revel in vulgarity for its own sake. Accents and voices underwent a change. It became stylish to seek out the meretricious in human affairs as a desirable value, an aim. Behaviour veered towards the raffish, and the emperor started to lose what little was left of his ancient sense of humour. It subtly modified his taste in sexual exchange — pain, erotic cruelty began to be sought out, and slaves were officially encouraged to seek out new forms of gratification to fathom the desires of old voluptuaries who in the past were circumspect and choice in their passions. All this we hoped that Cunégonde would cure with her rubber sheath worn as a safeguard against AIDS. The emperor called it 'Life in the Bithynian style.' I could not quite forget that he had once been a civil servant of merit, a functionary of high standing, renowned for his utter trustworthiness. What went wrong we shall presumably never know for certain — they had once shared everything down to their boys with all their skin infections. Exchanged verses and epigrams. Did Agrippa come between them in some inscrutable way? It is one version of the story, though quite insubstantial as yet."

* * *

PETITES ANNONCES
(From Cunégonde's matrimonial agency)

Mesopotamian lady without arms or legs wishes to encounter legless man of general culture to start a new life. Pressure cooker desirable but not indispensable.

Véritable Turc en amour vous offre expérience gratuite.

Superb witch-spinster offers lessons in good breeding for modest cash reward.

Lustful janisarry offers Turkish delight for reasonable reward.

Nonchalant Armenian gentleman *ressemblant* Rupert Brooke, seeks soul-mate.

Faux-jeton confirmé, vieux loup de mer flambé au pastis, riche mais casse-pieds, cherche compagne faramineuse. Moins de 10 ans s'abstenir.

Très achevée cruciverbiste, endiablée bonne à tous rapports, cherche à fonder foyer.

Provence

Jeune cadre sympa, tonique et très actuel, cherche jeune femme pour activité sympa.

Rancid old fakir seeks disciples unavoidably soiled.

Poète vend sa femme en viager, cherche belle trépannée soumise.

*   *   *

As for the poet . . .

Now, with the Principle of Indeterminacy together with the Identity of Opposites becoming the common currency of our thinking, Reality has become provisional and tentative. There is no such thing as a stable fact in all nature. Everything is subject to qualification. The primacy of poetry regarded as the distributor of psychic truth seems in doubt. A hilarious inconsequence appears to rule nature now. Putting words down on paper in a specific order results in a merciless lampoon of reality. The poem is a linguistic freak, a parody of what was once a religious act of magic, controlling dumb time by special breathing (yoga). An act of grace. The poet must now be prepared to specialize in the unforeseeable, to co-operate with the inevitable, to tinker with it, to tamper with Total Time. His poem is the site of a pure improbability, the hinge of a new fruitfulness, the fatal *déclic* of an orgasm which provokes a pure prismatic realization within the code of a normative reality which promises to translate the predictions of the liar-dice. But he faces an experience impossible to describe because of the inadequacies of language itself. Nevertheless by trying, by taking up the poetic posture, the Hindu asana, something magical happens (not always). He pivots reality and reorients it towards a new psychic epicentre, an opening on THE REAL NEWS, a bewitching ikon of all time. The obviously superb version of nature intervenes, and with it the Socratic Voice begins to compile its secret and cryptic chronicles of space and time. With this comes a glimpse of the griefless state, the grimaces of pure love!

POEM SURE POEM AS AN OPEN DOOR

POEM SURE SOMETHING HE HAS WAITED FOR

Never forget the last words of Aristotle: *"Si vous ne branchez pas votre rasoir électrique dans le cul d'un sage vous ne serez jamais bien rasé."*

The last specimen of Poet is kept on a reserve in America, visited daily by scientists who take his blood pressure. He is a salaried man with nothing to worry about. *C'est l'homme qui a rendu le suicide pleinement rentable.* A thought for a doggie-bag. Poems come inadvertently. "An ant may imagine a sugar lump as a whole but can only carry it away grain by grain."

*   *   *

"It was Friday the thirteenth and they were coming to measure me for a coffin. How peaceful the world seemed, undertakers were resolute and well set up men with the paunches of equerries. I could see them eyeing me for weight. But when I poured them out a glass of Macon they smiled thoughtfully and drank with relish and stealth. One said that it would be an insult to the memory of his father (a Macon man) to drink it carelessly; but the other said that he had always been a sloshpot and he was not going to change so late in life. And so the deed was done and the assistant presented a contract in italics which, if you signed it, was a guarantee that you would not be eaten by cockroaches in primal slumber or buggered by djinns."

Poem of a discrete ego

In borrowed bodies love commits blackmail:
In forged particulars couples set sail,
With heart-on-sleeve, with love to no avail,

191

Provence

The Damocles of sex their oft-told tale,
With what's the usefulness which must prevail.
Fathom one lover's look and glean the whole
Rebuked by silence with its pure control.

How lucky I was to have a companion like Cunégonde to record my observations as life lived itself away in time-consuming shudders in the lifeless historic crater, once an ornament of human history — that fatal illusion. Yes, the idea of history as a linear progression of events is in doubt, for history proceeds in little clicks of realization, intuitions. You have christened them Mnemons after the Goddess of Memory, the ancient Mnemosyne. They are ideograms for knowledge, the whole of knowledge. Little chirps from the wistful archaic bird of thought. Poems which carry the true signature. For example, one such real event was when in the First Quarto of *Hamlet* our Hero signs his message with the phrase *"Whilst this Machine is to him,* Hamlet." The European psyche registered a little hop of true history here, a change of epicentre recorded itself! Machine!

Whole sections of the ancient civilization have escaped contamination and it is sufficient to run a robot with a *pifomètre* over them to find out which can still support life unpoisoned by radioactive rayons. For example, we shall for some time (until the final checks are harmonized by the computers) be forced to limit ourselves to the somewhat insipid but guilt-free tin of Jewish Mother's Chicken Noodle Soup: "Prepared by licensed rabbis in accordance with age-old hygienic principles in two top synagogues in Hollywood. The only certain cure for AIDS!"

The Romans were right. "Boredom is infinitely more powerful than love!" But in this case what has become increasingly obvious is that a whole civilization must be reinvented, must be thought out anew. What form must it take? Something founded in error, founded in Poetry — last of the great blood-sports? We know no other way than by this anachronistic path via the ancient forms of simplicity. The poet is someone who is not rotting on the branch. Indeed anyone who strays into the magnetic field which will turn him into a poet is aware of a shock equal to a sort of life commitment. It is like having a baby — he is enslaved by the promise of a new insight. No further free choice is possible on this vector. It is like having one's blood changed to musk — you become a Polyhedral Person full of the airs and graces of your native language! Now the only hairshirt and thumbscrew for the real poet is the horrible conviviality of talentless tosspots who won't take yes for an answer! A good poet is always in training for the next life but three. That is why he has that pale, posthumous look. Yet always ready to seize the Abrupt Path between two tantric breaths!

For the poet the irreversible shock marks a definitive change of consciousness. Suddenly the bloody thing is there, and has to be swallowed like three toads. In my case I had to take into account a heliocentric Muse with lunar leanings. I dealt with it somewhat summarily in my pamphlet *How to keep quite still inside* or *How to prevent your elephant cheating at cards*. And love? Why, love breaks in when you can sign your letters *"Indécrottablement vôtre"* and *"très profondément dépressif,"* which will show how high up you are on death's wanted list. Dear Cunégonde smiles her slow Latex smile when she hears this. She has realized so much about human love since she was dipped in the rubber love-bath in order to take on her present enchanting form. I write her a statutory love-letter . . .

"Dear Cuné,
I don't want you to fade away into pure supposition but to bear witness to the existence of a science of bliss through love, with no limitation of age or sex. Dear old exonerated jujube for whom all is Jam, hearken to my words: peace like

love or lust is always there to be exuded or eluded or both if you bear in mind that things will begin to concern you when they start to matter not at all — when they cease to matter. Zero becomes mysteriously 'love' in tennis. Remember the Arabs brought it into Maths to help with the arch of their mosques! Later came Petrarch and Laura and the natural history of the human sigh. The residual life has now become posthumous, you might say."

Also sprach little Cunégonde . . .

She says, "The poet best exercises his demonic function by shutting up and trusting to the automatic pilot, but this is hard to learn unless one has been trained as a fisherman and knows how to wait. Like a good cook: *L'art d'accommoder les restes!* The bore is that one is forbidden to be explicit: anything that can be explained or codified has missed the point; hasn't been experienced. It has grazed the Thing meant, the target which must be approached tangentially, obliquely, be inferred."

Pause here for a disenfranchised sob! My rubber wife and I
exchange unexpended tears at night, by the light of a humble
candle, on a mountain of ash and dead slag.
Watching all time quietly elapse
Into a sort of great Perhaps
Fluid yet uniform: no gaps
A womb without a real prolapse.

C'est la mort qui grimace tendrement.

Living an a-historical life
Writing love-letters to the world's wife
In invisible ink once you reach the Brink
Watch for the slip twixt fuck and think.

194

Or else I give her a lecture on mineral love by the light of
Descartes and Company . . .

Le cercle refermé

Boom of the sunset gun
In the old fortress at Benares,
And a single sobbing bugle calls
The naphtha flares on river craft
Corpses floating skyward
The thumbworship of the dead
Gnomes with their vast collisions
Of water and weed and light
With the dead awake all night
The coffined dead true in love's despite
The thumbscrews of awareness screwed in tight.

The girl with nine wombs is there to chide
What does it mean, your ancient loneliness?
Today they are coming to measure me for a coffin,
So dying you begin to sleepwalk and regain your youth.

Mere time is winding down at last:
The consenting harvest moon presides,
Appears on cue to hold our hearts in fee,
The genetics of our doubts holds fast
And a carotid is haunted by old caresses
The caresses of silence.
When young and big with poems
Caressed by my heliocentric muse
With lunar leanings, I was crafty in loving,
Or jaunty as a god of the bullfrogs
The uncanny promptings of the human I.

Provence

Love-babies nourished by the sigh,
With little thought of joy or pain,
Or the spicy Kodak of the hangman's brain
A disenfranchised last goodbye,
                    Goodbye.

Notes and Sources

Among classical sources I have drawn mainly on Ausonius, Celsus, Euxinus, Galen, Julian, Livy, Minucius Felix, Petronius, Plutarch, Suetonius and Tacitus. Apart from standard reference works and guide books I have consulted or quoted from the following:

Baring-Gould, S., *In Troubadour-Land*, London, 1891
Busquet, Raoul, V. L. Bourrilly and M. Agulhon, *Histoire de la Provence*, Paris, 1972
Chardenon, Ludo, *Mémoires et Recettes de Ludo Chardenon*, (Ramasseur de Plantes Languedocien), Avignon/Le Paradou, 1982
————, *In Praise of Wild Herbs*, London 1985
Cook, Theodore Andrea, *Old Provence*, London, 1905
Forster, E. M., *Alexandria: A History and Guide*, Alexandria, 1922; edited by Michael Haag, London, 1982
Grant, Michael, *Cleopatra*, London, 1972
Lafitte-Houssat, Jacques, *Troubadours et Cours d'Amour*, Paris, 1950
Hare, Augustus J. C., *South-Eastern France*, London, 1890
Kazantzakis, Nikos, *Report to Greco*, translated by Peter Bien, London, 1965
Lenthéric, Charles, *La Grèce et L'Orient en Provence*, Paris, 1878
The Memoirs of Frédéric Mistral, translated by George Wickes, New York, 1986

Provence

Nelli, René, *L'Erotique des Troubadours*, Toulouse, 1963

de Rougemont, Denis, *Passion and Society*, translated by Montgomery Belgion, London, 1940; revised 1956

Stendhal, *De l'Amour*, Paris, 1822 and *Mémoires d'un Touriste*, Paris, 1838

Symonds, John Addington, *Sketches in Italy and Greece*, London, 1874

The Complete Letters of Vincent van Gogh, translated by J. van Gogh-Bonger and C. de Dood, London, 1958

Lettres de Vincent van Gogh à son frère Théo, Paris, 1986

List of Poems

"There is still a great deal of Greece all through the Tartarin and Daumier part of this queer country, where the good folk have the accent you know; there is a Venus of Arles just as there is a Venus of Lesbos, and one still feels the youth of it in spite of all. I haven't the slightest doubt that some day you too will know the Midi."*

— Vincent van Gogh to his brother Theo,
Arles, September 1888

*Translation by J. van Gogh-Bonger and C. de Dood, from *The Complete Letters of Vincent van Gogh*, 1958